The Chinese Grammar Wiki

BOOK:

Just the Basics

The Chinese Grammar Wiki
BOOK:

Just the Basics

Editor-in-Chief John Pasden

Foreword by Dr. David Moser

SHANGHAI

Published by AllSet Learning, Shanghai, China.

For information about educational or bulk purchases, please contact AllSet Learning at
sales@allsetlearning.com.

1st print edition, 2018.

Paperback ISBN: 978-1-941875-38-4
eBook ISBN: 978-1-941875-37-7
ASID: 20180323T122038

The Chinese Grammar Wiki is a trademark of AllSet Learning.

For anyone who ever tried
to learn Chinese and thought,
"there has to be an easier way."

Table of Contents

Foreword   1

Introduction   3

Chinese Grammar Basics for Beginners   4

Basic Sentence Order   12

Time Words and Word Order   15

Indicating Location with 在 (zai) Before Verbs   17

The 'Also' Adverb 也 (ye)   19

Simple 'Noun + Adjective' Sentences   24

Tag Questions with 吗 (ma)   27

Questions with 呢 (ne)   29

Placement of Question Words   32

Expressing Possession with 的 (de)   43

Expressing Possession with 有 (you)   45

Standard Negation with 不 (bu)   47

Negation of 有 (you) with 没 (mei)   50

Connecting Nouns with 是 (shi)   53

Expressing Existence in a Place with 在 (zai)   56

Expressing Existence with 有 (you)   58

Using the Verb 叫 (jiao)   60

Using the Verb 去 (qu)   62

The 'All' Adverb 都 (dou)   65

Expressing 'Excessively' with 太 (tai)   67

Expressing 'And' with 和 (he)   69

Offering Choices with 还是 (haishi)   71

Structure of Numbers   73

Structure of Times (Basic)   79

Structure of Days of the Week   82

Foreword

Learning Chinese used to be a frustratingly "front-loaded" endeavor. One had to first learn Pinyin, the four tones, how to write thousands of characters with the correct stroke order, how to use the 214 radicals to look up unfamiliar characters in a dictionary, and, of course, how to limn the mysterious principles of Chinese grammar. This process entailed inordinate sacrifices of eyesight, friends, and years of precious life spent "learning to learn Chinese," before the hapless student could be weaned from a diet of pre-digested pabulum and delve into the messy, glorious world of real texts.

The Chinese Grammar Wiki is on the cutting edge of a growing arsenal of digital and Web resources that have made this front-loaded Sisyphean nightmare a thing of the past. This very cool tool, developed by John Pasden and the folks at AllSet Learning, is in accordance with the new "learning grammar as you go" principle of Chinese study in the digital age. Learners can now boldly embark on the ocean of Chinese very early on, with navigational tools like the Grammar Wiki to reduce the risk of getting lost at sea. For the intrepid, motivated learner, studying Chinese can now be an adventure, instead of a five-year stint in solitary confinement. And from the very outset, students can begin to move toward the goal that was formerly so elusive: the acquisition of 语感 (yǔgǎn), the "feeling for the language."

In my opinion, the Chinese Grammar Wiki has at least three very strong characteristics:

Modularity. This is a long-standing commonsense feature of website design, but it's absolutely crucial for a grammar tool like this. The Wiki has conveniently carved up Chinese grammar into useful modular chunks with the beginner in mind, so that searching for a structure or topic is intuitive, quick, and yields a clear explanation that enables the user to forge ahead, enlightened and empowered. The structure and site map is user-friendly at every level, which means that the Wiki can be easily "plugged in" to existing Chinese syllabi, or simply employed by the student independently to explore texts and materials outside of class.

Interlinking. The Wiki is structured so that alongside the grammar points on most pages there are helpful links to related or similar grammar points within the Wiki. For example, in exploring the grammatical points for 比 (bǐ) involving comparison, you will find explanations of the basic 比 (bǐ) structure, examples, and common errors, but in addition you will also see links to other "comparison" structures using 没有 (méiyǒu). This interlinking feature gives the user a fuller picture of various grammatical structures that serve similar functions in the language.

Universality. One of the strongest points of the Chinese Grammar Wiki is that the grammatical explanations have been tailored so as to contain the right amount of information, at the right level of specificity and complexity for the majority of learners. Designing a grammar resource with such wide applicability is not an easy task, requiring not only technical know-how and careful thinking, but also a strong intuitive sense of what the average student needs to know. Linguist Edward Sapir said "all grammars leak," and this mutable, watery quality of language means that no grammatical framework is going to contain only tidy, airtight rules that cover every situation. In explanations, there is always a tradeoff between succinct simplicity and the real-life complexity, and the wiki does an admirable job of striking a satisfying balance between these two yin-yang poles.

Being digital in nature, the Chinese Grammar Wiki is very much a work in progress, and the designers always welcome input and suggestions. Product development is always an interactive process, and the more people use the resource, the more useful it will become. I encourage Chinese students at all levels – and even Chinese teachers – to check it out and discover what the reference tools of the 21st century will look like.

No matter what well-meaning pedagogical Pollyannas might tell you, Chinese is still "damn hard." Thankfully, there now are digital resources like the Chinese Grammar Wiki, which goes a long way to making the struggle easier.

David Moser
Academic Director, CET Beijing Chinese Studies
Beijing Capital Normal University

Introduction

The **Chinese Grammar Wiki** began life as an Excel spreadsheet full of grammar points organized by difficulty level. This list was needed to track the progress of AllSet Learning's clients and to design personalized grammar practice where it was most needed. But as the lists continued to grow and evolve, it quickly became apparent that it made sense to put the grammar points online, so that the newest version would always be front and center. For ease of editing, what could be better than a wiki? And if AllSet Learning teachers were to have access, why not open up access to *all learners*? The Chinese Grammar Wiki was developed internally for about a year before becoming public in January of 2012. Since then, it has grown tremendously, both in content and in traffic.

Probably the most important feature of the Chinese Grammar Wiki, which has always been kept at the forefront of its development, is its focus on learner level. An absolute beginner can't absorb a multitude of uses for every grammar point she encounters, and she shouldn't be expected to. And she certainly shouldn't be given frustratingly difficult example sentences when trying to grasp the most basic grammar concepts. That's why example sentences on the Chinese Grammar Wiki are plentiful, but relentlessly edited to be level-appropriate. And for the learners that can't get enough, relevant articles of all levels are always just a link away. Although the wiki aims to be 100% comprehensive, it's no coincidence that there are fewer A1 grammar points than A2 grammar points, and fewer A2 grammar points than B1 grammar points. Considerable thought and care has gone into curating and pruning the lists of grammar points.

The Chinese Grammar Wiki is not a Chinese course. Rather, it is a companion resource that can complement any Chinese class. Don't expect to read it from start to finish, or to go through the grammar point lists from top to bottom. But do expect to come back often. And expect to get sucked into the curiously logical world of Chinese grammar.

John Pasden
Editor-in-Chief and CEO
AllSet Learning, Shanghai, China

Beginner Guide to Chinese Grammar

As a beginner, Chinese grammar can be challenging to understand. In this quick overview, we will provide you with some basic information on Chinese grammar as well as some good starting points.

Background

English is classified as an Indo-European language. This language family includes a lot of languages spoken in the western world, including the romance languages (such as Spanish, French, and Portuguese) as well as the Slavic languages (such as Russian, Czech, and Polish), and many others. All of these languages have common grammatical features which include conjugating verbs for different tenses, following specific rules about subject-verb agreement, and adding endings to words to make them plural.

Chinese is not part of the Indo-European family at all. Instead, it is classified as a Sino-Tibetan language, and, unsurprisingly, its grammar is quite different from the grammar of those European languages you may have encountered before. Still, Chinese grammar may surprise you with its pleasing simplicity and consistent logical structure.

As a language, Chinese (quote famously) does not have an alphabet. Instead, characters known as "*hanzi*" (汉字) are used to express the different sounds of the language. These characters can also be written using the roman letters in a system called "pinyin." All beginners should learn pinyin first. Pinyin is provided for all Chinese characters that appear in A1 and A2 grammar points.

The Basics

There are a number of misconceptions about Chinese grammar, the most egregious being that "Chinese has no grammar." If Mandarin Chinese truly had *no grammar*, you could make no grammar mistakes, and no learners would ever struggle with it. We will start this overview by looking at some specific areas of Chinese grammar that can sometimes trip up beginners.

Word Order

For many simple cases, the basic sentence structure[1] of Chinese is the same in Chinese as it is in English. Both languages use a subject-verb or subject-verb-object (SVO) formula for making simple sentences. This familiar pattern means that you shouldn't have much trouble with word order at first.

---

1. Basic sentence order (A1), page 12

Subject-Verb Examples:

Subject	Verb	Translation
你 Nǐ	吃。 chī.	You eat.
他 Tā	笑。 xiào.	He laughs.
我 Wǒ	去。 qù.	I go.

Subject-Verb-Object Examples:

	Subject	Verb	Object	Translation
▷	我 Wǒ	吃。 chī.	肉。 ròu.	I eat meat.
▷	你 Nǐ	喝 hē	水。 shuǐ.	You drink water.
▷	他 Tā	说 shuō	中文。 Zhōngwén.	He speaks Chinese.

More examples can be found on our <u>basic word order</u>[1] page.

As sentences get more complex, you'll note that Chinese word order does, in fact, diverge significantly from English word order, even for some relatively simple sentences. For help with those, check out our articles on <u>time words</u>[2], <u>locations of actions</u>[3], using <u>simple adverbs correctly</u>[4], and making <u>simple noun-adjective sentences</u>[5].

Questions

Simple sentences can be turned into yes/no questions by adding <u>吗 (ma)</u>[6] to the end of simple statements. For each of the following, you could make a simple statement by dropping 吗 (ma).

---

1. Basic sentence order (A1), page 12
2. Time words and word order (A2), page 15
3. Indicating location with "zai" before verbs (A2), page 17
4. The "also" adverb "ye" (A1), page 19
5. Simple "noun + adjective" sentences (A1), page 24
6. Tag questions with "ma" (A1), page 27

他是老师 吗 ？
question

Tā shì lǎoshī ma ？

Is he a teacher?

你喜欢咖啡 吗 ？
question

Nǐ xǐhuan kāfēi ma ？

Do you like coffee?

他是机器人 吗 ？
question

Tā shì jīqìrén ma ？

Is he a robot?

Another important question particle for beginners to understand is 呢 (ne)[1]. 呢 (ne) is simply added after a topic to turn it into a "what about...?" question. This is useful in conversations to say things like "what about you?" or "what about my money?" This particle is simply tagged onto a subject to form the question.

我吃饭了。你 呢 ？

Wǒ chīfàn le. Nǐ ne ？

I've eaten. What about you?

北京下雨了。上海 呢 ？

Běijīng xià yǔ le. Shànghǎi ne ？

It's raining in Beijing. How about Shanghai?

你说他们可以去。我们 呢 ？

Nǐ shuō tāmen kěyǐ qù. Wǒmen ne ？

You said they can go. What about us?

There are of course other ways to form questions[2]. In English, we use question words, commonly referred to as the "5 W's and 1 H" (what, where, who, when, why, how), to make questions. These question words also exist in Chinese, but their placement within a sentence in Chinese is different from English. The structure of a question in Chinese follows the same structure as a normal statement.

For example, in English the structure of the question "Who are you?" puts the question word "who" at the beginning of the sentence. If the person answering this question says, "I am Li Li" we can see that the answer to the question comes at the end of the sentence. In Chinese, the structure of the question to learn someone's name is "You are who?" So the question follows the same structure as the answer (subject-verb-object). This works for all kinds of other

---

1. Questions with "ne" (A1), page 29
2. Placement of question words (A1), page 32

questions too. For example, in Chinese, to ask "What is it?" you literally say, "It is what?"

- 什么

  shénme

  what

- 哪里 / 哪儿

  nǎlǐ / nǎr

  where

- 谁

  shéi

  who

- 什么时候

  shénme shíhou

  when

- 为什么

  wèishénme

  why

- 怎么

  zěnme

  how

Possession

Possession can be shown using the particle 的 (de)[1]. This character functions the same way as an apostrophe-"s" does in English and is added after the "owner," before the "thing owned." One interesting result of this extremely versatile system is that you don't need separate words for "my" or "your" or "his"; you just follow the words for "I" or "you" or "he" with a 的 (de).

▷ • 小李 的 手机

  Xiǎo Lǐ de shǒujī

  Xiao Li's cell phone

▷ • 我 的 手机

  Wǒ de shǒujī

  My cell phone

---

1. Expressing possession with "de" (A1), page 43

- 公司 的 老板

  gōngsī de lǎobǎn

  the company's boss

- 他 的 小狗

  Tā de xiǎogǒu

  His puppy

Possession can also be expressed with 有 (yǒu)[1], the Chinese verb meaning "to have." Just like we can say in English "I have the tickets" or "she has the camera," 有 (yǒu) can indicate this type of possession.

- 我 有 钱。

  Wǒ yǒu qián.

  I have money.

▷ 他 有 两个女儿。

  Tā yǒu liǎng gè nǚér.

  He has two daughters.

▷ 你 有 工作吗?

  Nǐ yǒu gōngzuò ma?

  Do you have a job?

Negation

The same basic word order holds true when using the negative. Simply put the word 不 (bù)[2] before verbs[2] and adjectives[2]. This functions much like the word "not" in English.

- 我 不 喝酒 。

  bù hējiǔ.

  She doesn't drink alcohol.

▷ 他们 不 想工作 。

  Tāmen bù xiǎng gōngzuò .

  They don't want to work.

- 她 不 漂亮 。

  Tā bù piàoliang .

  She is not pretty.

---

1. Expressing possession with "you" (A1), page 45
2. Standard negation with "bu" (A1), page 47

When talking about what you do not "have," you use the word 没 (méi)[1] instead of 不 (bu). It is placed right before the verb 有 (yǒu)[2] to form the "do not have" phrase 没有 (méiyǒu)[1]. This allows you to say sentences like "Walter doesn't have a car" or "Voltron doesn't have the books."

▷ 我 没 有 手机。

Wǒ méi yǒu shǒujī.

I don't have a cell phone.

• 我们 没 有 房子。

Wǒmen méi yǒu fángzi.

We don't have a house.

• 他们公司 没 有 电脑。

Tāmen gōngsī méi yǒu diànnǎo.

Their company doesn't have computers.

Aspect

As we mentioned already, there is a silly notion floating around that Chinese has no grammar. While this belief is false, it probably stems from the fact Chinese has no formal tenses to express events that took place in either the past or the future. Instead of tense, the language makes use of time words[3] and puts more emphasis on aspect. You don't need to worry about this in the beginning; just remember to use time words to make clear when something happened, and the aspect thing will come with time. (Hint: aspect involves the particle 了 (le), which you'll be spending more time with later.)

Parts of Speech

All words can be classified into parts of speech to define what roles the words play in sentences. Here, we will briefly recap how these different parts of speech work in English, and explain how the same rules apply to Chinese grammar.

Nouns are commonly referred to as "person, place, or thing" words. As you start learning more Chinese vocabulary, many of the words you will learn will be nouns. These will make up the subjects and the objects of the sentences you study.

Verbs are words that describe actions (sometimes mental or abstract rather than physical). Chinese does not conjugate verbs. Chinese verbs stay the same, regardless of when the action takes place or who performs it.

---

1. Negation of "you" with "mei" (A1), page 50
2. Expressing possession with "you" (A1), page 45
3. Time words and word order (A2), page 15

Here are some good verbs for beginners to start learning:

- 是 (shì) - verb for "to be"[1]
- 在 (zài) - verb for "to be located"[2]
- 有 (yǒu) - verb for "there is / there are"[3]
- 叫 (jiào) - verb for "to be called"[4]
- 去 (qù) - verb for "to go"[5]

Adverbs are words that modify verbs and adjectives. In Chinese, the adverb *always* goes *before* the verb or adjective. Instead of saying "I run also," proper grammar in Chinese would be "I also run." It's very consistent in Chinese.

Here are some good adverbs for beginners to start learning:

- 都 (dōu) - adverb for "all"[6]
- 也 (yě) - adverb for "also"[7]
- 太 (tài) - adverb for "too," as in "excessively"[8]

Adjectives are words that describe nouns. Chinese has some unique rules about how adjectives interact with different nouns and verbs.

Here are some good adjective rules for beginners to start learning:

- Simple sentences with adjectives[9]
- 是 (shì) - the verb for "to be"[1]

Conjunctions are words that join two thoughts together in a sentence. The three most common ones in English are "and," "but," and "or." As you learn more about these conjunctions in Chinese, you will discover that they're each a little different from their English equivalents.

Here are some good conjunctions for beginners to start learning:

- 和 (hé) - conjunction for "and"[10]
- 还是 (háishì) - conjunction for "or"[11]

---

1. Connecting nouns with "shi" (A1), page 53
2. Expressing existence in a place with "zai" (A1), page 56
3. Expressing existence with "you" (A1), page 58
4. Using the verb "jiao" (A1), page 60
5. Using the verb "qu" (A1), page 62
6. The "all" adverb "dou" (A1), page 65
7. The "also" adverb "ye" (A1), page 19
8. Expressing "excessively" with "tai" (A1), page 67
9. Simple "noun + adjective" sentences (A1), page 24
10. Expressing "and" with "he" (A1), page 69
11. Offering choices with "haishi" (A1), page 71

Articles are kind of a confusing concept in English, but the main English articles are "a," "an," and "the." We use them when saying things like "I have a laptop" or "open the door." In Chinese, articles *don't exist*. There is no word for "a" or "the" in Chinese.

Numbers are the words we use to express specific quantities. We use numbers to express value, time, and other important functions in our lives. They can be used for all of these same functions in Chinese.

Here are some good number structures for beginners to start learning.

- Structure of numbers[1]
- Structure of times[2]
- Structure of days of the week[3]
- Structure of dates[4]

Measure words are words that pair up with numbers and help describe the nouns that are being counted (or "measured"). We don't have such a pervasive, complete system for this in English, but we do something similar when we say, "5 pieces of pizza" or "3 sheets of paper."

Here is the only measure word beginners need to start learning the concept:

- Measure word 个 (gè)[5]

Ready for more?

Of course all of this is just the beginning. There are many more interesting grammar patterns that can help you correctly express lots of different things in Chinese. Take a look at the A1 grammar points for more beginner-friendly grammar help. Just keep in mind that these grammar points are not sequential. Start with what you need help with most, and branch out from there.

---

1. Structure of numbers (A1), page 73
2. Structure of times (basic) (A1), page 79
3. Structure of days of the week (A1), page 82
4. Structure of dates (A1), page 85
5. Measure word "ge" (A1), page 87

Basic sentence order (A1)

In its most basic form, Chinese word order is very similar to English word order. These similarities definitely have their limits, though; don't expect the two languages' word orders to stay consistent much beyond the very basic sentence orders outlined below.

Subject-Predicate

A simple predicate can be just a verb. The most basic word order in Chinese is:

Structure

Subj. + Verb

You can form very simple sentences with just two words.

Examples

Subject	Verb	Translation
你们 Nǐmen	吃。 chī.	You eat.
他 Tā	笑。 xiào.	He laughs.
我 Wǒ	读。 dú.	I read.
你 Nǐ	去。 qù.	You go.
你们 Nǐmen	看。 kàn.	You look.
你 Nǐ	来。 lái.	You come here!
我 Wǒ	说。 shuō.	I speak.
孩子 Háizi	哭。 kū.	Children cry.

谁 Shéi	要学? yào xué?	Who wants to study?
谁 Shéi	想玩? xiǎng wán?	Who wants to play?

Subject-Verb-Object

A slightly longer predicate might be a verb with an object. A sentence with both a verb and an object is formed with this structure:

Structure

Subj. + Verb + Obj.

This is the same as in English, and is commonly referred to as SVO word order. You can express a huge variety of things with this simple structure.

Examples

Subject	Verb	Object	Translation
他们 Tāmen	吃 chī	肉。 ròu.	They eat meat.
你 Nǐ	喝 hē	茶吗? chá ma?	Do you drink tea?
我 Wǒ	去 qù	学校。 xuéxiào.	I go to school.
他 Tā	说 shuō	中文。 Zhōngwén.	He speaks Chinese.
你 Nǐ	喜欢 xǐhuan	孩子吗? háizi ma?	Do you like kids?
我们 Wǒmen	要买 yào mǎi	电脑。 diànnǎo.	We want to buy a computer.
你们 Nǐmen	想吃 xiǎng chī	中国菜吗? Zhōngguó cài ma?	Do you want to eat Chinese food?

我 Wǒ	爱 ài	你和爸爸。 nǐ hé bàba.	I love you and dad.
他们 Tāmen	要做 yào zuò	什么? shénme?	What do they want to do?
你 Nǐ	想去 xiǎng qù	什么地方? shénme dìfang?	What place do you want to go to?

When Things Get Tricky

Despite the convenient word order similarities highlighted above, things start to break down as soon as you start adding in such simple sentence elements as the "also" adverb 也 (yě)[1], a time word[2], or a location where something happened[3].

Don't worry; the more complicated Chinese structures aren't hard, they're just different! (If Chinese word order were really the same as English word order, that would be just a little too convenient, wouldn't it?)

Similar to

- Connecting nouns with "shi" (A1), page 53

- Placement of question words (A1), page 32

- Simple "noun + adjective" sentences (A1), page 24

- Standard negation with "bu" (A1), page 47

- Wanting to do something with "yao"

- Actions in a row

- Indicating location with "zai" before verbs (A2), page 17

---

1. The "also" adverb "ye" (A1), page 19
2. Time words and word order (A2), page 15
3. Indicating location with "zai" before verbs (A2), page 17

Time words and word order (A2)

Remembering where to put the time words, such as "yesterday," "tomorrow," "this week," etc. in a sentence is really important in order to speak Chinese correctly. In Chinese you get two equally correct choices.

Structure

Time words can appear in one of two positions in the sentence in Chinese: either at the beginning of the sentence (before the subject), or directly after the subject. The structures are:

> **Time** + Subj. + Verb + Obj.

> Subj. + **Time** + Verb + Obj.

So if you start speaking with "time first" English word order, you can carry on and get away with it. If, however, you're saving the time word for the *end* of the sentence, you can be pretty sure that it doesn't sound at all natural to your Chinese audience.

Examples

 昨天 我 去了酒吧。

Zuótiān wǒ qù le jiǔbā.

Yesterday I went to the bar.

• 我 昨天 去了酒吧。

Wǒ zuótiān qù le jiǔbā.

I went to the bar yesterday.

 下个星期 他 要回国。

Xià gè xīngqī tā yào huí guó.

Next week he is going back to his country.

• 他 下个星期 要回国。

Tā xià gè xīngqī yào huí guó.

He is going back to his country next week.

▷ 明年 我 要开一个公司。

Míngnián wǒ yào kāi yī gè gōngsī.

Next year I want to open a company.

◦ 我 明年 要开一个公司。

Wǒ míngnián yào kāi yī gè gōngsī.

I want to open a company next year.

◦ 下个月 我们 结婚吧?

Xià gè yuè wǒmen jiéhūn ba?

Next month shall we get married?

◦ 我们 下个月 结婚吧?

Wǒmen xià gè yuè jiéhūn ba?

Shall we get married next month?

◦ 现在 你 能来我办公室吗?

Xiànzài nǐ néng lái wǒ bàngōngshì ma?

Now you can come to my office?

◦ 你 现在 能来我办公室吗?

Nǐ xiànzài néng lái wǒ bàngōngshì ma?

Can you come to my office now?

Similar to

- Basic sentence order (A1), page 12

- Wanting to do something with "yao"

Indicating location with "zai" before verbs (A2)

If you need to include the place where an action takes place, you can use
在 (zài). Just pay close attention to <u>word order</u>₁, as this is one case in which
Chinese word order is quite different from English.

Structure

To indicate the location that a verb takes place in, 在 (zài), followed by a location, comes before the verb.

Notice that the location is placed *before* the verb in Chinese, whereas in English it appears *afterwards*.

Examples

▷ 我 在 上海 上大学。

Wǒ zài Shànghǎi shàng dàxué.

I went to college in Shanghai.

▷ 你一直 在 这家公司 工作吗?

Nǐ yīzhí zài zhè jiā gōngsī gōngzuò ma?

Have you always been working in this company?

* 我周末想 在 家 睡觉。

Wǒ zhōumò xiǎng zài jiā shuìjiào.

On the weekend, I want to sleep at home.

▷ 不要 在 床上 吃东西。

Bù yào zài chuáng shàng chī dōngxi.

Don't eat food on the bed.

* 你想 在 哪儿 开生日派对?

Nǐ xiǎng zài nǎr kāi shēngrì pàiduì?

Where do you want to have the birthday party?

---

1. Basic sentence order (A1), page 12

- 他喜欢 在 厕所里 抽烟。

  Tā xǐhuan zài cèsuǒ lǐ chōuyān.

  He likes to smoke in the bathroom.

- 很多人 在 地铁上 吃早饭。

  Hěn duō rén zài dìtiě shàng chī zǎofàn.

  Many people eat breakfast on the subway.

- 现在我们 在 KTV 唱歌。

  Xiànzài wǒmen zài KTV chànggē.

  Now we're singing songs at karaoke.

- 老板 在 会议室 见客户。

  Lǎobǎn zài huìyìshì jiàn kèhù.

  The boss is seeing the client in the meeting room.

- 你 在 外面 吃过晚饭了吗?

  Nǐ zài wàimiàn chī guo wǎnfàn le ma?

  Did you eat dinner outside?

Remember: in English we usually put the location at the end of a sentence. In Chinese, we put the location after the subject but *before* the verb.

Getting More Specific with Locations

Rather than just using 在 (zài) to mean "at" a location, you might want to use it to mean "in," "on," or "under" a specific location. To do this, you'll need to add an extra word after the location. Learn about expressing location with "zai… shang / xia / li".

Similar to

- Basic sentence order (A1), page 12

- Expressing existence in a place with "zai" (A1), page 56

- Expressing location with "zai… shang / xia / li"

- Special cases of "zai" following verbs

- Time words and word order (A2), page 15

- Using "dao" to mean "to go to"

The "also" adverb "ye" (A1)

The English adverb "too" or "also" is expressed in Chinese as 也 (yě). In Chinese, it *always* needs to come before the verb (or adjective).

也 (yě) with Verb Phrases

Structure

Since it is an adverb, 也 (yě) is inserted after the subject, before the verb or verb phrase.

 Subj. + 也 + Verb / [Verb Phrase]

Examples

▷ • 我 也 喜欢。

Wǒ yě xǐhuan.

I also like it.

▷ • 我 也 是学生。

Wǒ yě shì xuésheng.

I am a student too.

• 她 也 有一个儿子。

Tā yě yǒu yī gè érzi.

She also has a son.

• 他们 也 是法国人吗?

Tāmen yě shì Fǎguó rén ma?

Are they also French?

▷ • 我 也 想学中文。

Wǒ yě xiǎng xué Zhōngwén.

I also want to study Chinese.

• 他们 也 会去吗?

Tāmen yě huì qù ma?

Are they also going?

- 我妈妈 也 喜欢吃饺子。

  Wǒ māma yě xǐhuan chī jiǎozi.

  My mother likes to eat boiled dumplings too.

- 孩子 也 可以喝酒吗?

  Háizi yě kěyǐ hējiǔ ma?

  Can kids drink alcohol too?

- 你 也 想来我家吗?

  Nǐ yě xiǎng lái wǒ jiā ma?

  Do you want to come to my house too?

- 她 也 觉得这个老师不好。

  Tā yě juéde zhège lǎoshī bù hǎo.

  She also thinks this teacher isn't good.

Let's take one more look at two different English sentences which mean the same thing, but can result in bad Chinese if you translate word-for-word.

✔ 我 也 喜欢 。

Wǒ yě xǐhuan .

I also like it.

✘

Wǒ xǐhuan yě .

I like it too.

Note that the translation for the first sentence is "I also like it." The translation of the second sentence is "I like it too," which is equally correct in English, but translated word-for-word into Chinese, the 也 (yě) comes at the end of the sentence, which is *100% wrong* in Chinese.

A Note on the Negative Form

Please note that in English, we replace the word "too" with "either" in negative sentences. For example:

A: I like cats.

B: I like cats *too*.

A: I *don't* like cats.

B: I don't like cats *either*.

In Chinese, regardless of whether the sentence is positive ("I like them **too**") or negative ("I **don't** like them **either**"), 也 (yě) is used the same way. Just make sure you put the 也 (yě) *before* the 不 (bù) or other negative part that comes before the verb.

 我 也 不 喜欢。

Wǒ yě bù xǐhuan.

I don't like it either.

▷ 我 也 不 知道。

Wǒ yě bù zhīdào.

I don't know either.

▷ 他 也 没 有。

Tā yě méiyǒu.

He doesn't have it either.

• 你 也 不 想来我家吗?

Nǐ yě bù xiǎng lái wǒ jiā ma?

You don't want to come to my house either?

也 (yě) with Adjectives

Structure

也 (yě) can also be used with adjectives. Remember that for simple "noun + adjective" sentences[1] you normally need to include an adverb like 很 (hěn) before the adjective. In that case, just put the 也 (yě) before the adverb.

Subj. + 也 (+ Adv.) + Adj.

Examples

▷ 你 也 很 高。

Nǐ yě hěn gāo.

You are also tall.

• 他 也 很 胖。

Tā yě hěn pàng.

He is also fat.

---

1. Simple "noun + adjective" sentences (A1), page 24

- 我爸爸 也 很 帅。

  Wǒ bàba yě hěn shuài.

  My dad is also handsome.

▷ 湖南菜 也 很 辣。

  Húnán cài yě hěn là.

  Hunan food is very spicy too.

- 这种酒 也 很 好喝。

  Zhè zhǒng jiǔ yě hěn hǎohē.

  This kind of alcohol is also good.

- 这个地方 也 很 漂亮。

  Zhège dìfang yě hěn piàoliang.

  This place is also pretty.

- 昨天很冷，今天 也 很 冷。

  Zuótiān hěn lěng, jīntiān yě hěn lěng.

  Yesterday was cold, and today is also cold.

▷ 他生气了？我 也 很 生气！

  Tā shēngqì le? Wǒ yě hěn shēngqì!

  He got angry? I'm also angry!

▷ 这个问题 也 很 麻烦。

  Zhège wèntí yě hěn máfan.

  This problem is also very troublesome.

▷ 我觉得这个餐厅 也 很 好。

  Wǒ juéde zhège cāntīng yě hěn hǎo.

  I think that this restaurant is also good.

Expressing "Me Too" with 也 (yě)

It can be tricky to know how to say "me too" when you first study 也 (yě), as you can't say "wǒ yě" all by itself. That's not a complete sentence; you can't just leave 也 (yě) hanging there with nothing after it.

The all-purpose correct sentence is "wǒ yě shì," which literally means, "I am too," but can also stand in for "me too."

Structure

The correct structure uses the verb 是 (shì):

✔ 我 [也] [是] 。

Wǒ [yě] [shì] .

I am too. / Me too.

The 是 fills in for whatever was just said.

✘ 我 [也] 。

Wǒ [yě] .

Always put something after 也! It never ends a sentence.

Examples

The "me too" structure works with other subjects, as well. But for these simple examples, we'll stick to the classic 我 (wǒ) subject.

A: 我是美国人。

Wǒ shì Měiguó rén.

I am an American.
In addition to "在" you need a "上" to indicate the location "in the subway."

B: 我 [也] [是] 。

Wǒ [yě] [shì] .

Me too. / I am too.

For this next one, you'll notice that the "me too" reply repeats the original verb 喜欢 (xǐhuan) instead of using 是 (shì). Both ways are possible.

A: 我喜欢看书。

Wǒ xǐhuan kàn shū.

I like to read.

B: 我 [也] [喜欢] 。

Wǒ [yě] [xǐhuan] .

Me too. / So do I.

You'll notice that some of those English translations use "so do I." The Chinese works exactly the same; they're just translated that way to produce more natural-sounding English.

Similar to

- Simple "noun + adjective" sentences (A1), page 24

- Expressing "and also" with "hai"

- Using "ye" and "dou" together

Simple "noun + adjective" sentences (A1)

In English, nouns can be "linked" to adjectives and other nouns with the verb "to be." In Chinese, nouns are linked to other nouns in one way, but linked to adjectives in a completely different way. Nouns are linked to other <u>nouns with 是 (shì)</u>[1]. Nouns are linked to adjectives with 很 (hěn).

Structure

Noun + 很 + Adj.

The noun in this structure is the subject of the sentence. Sometimes the 很 (hěn) in this structure is translated as "very," but often it is just a way to link a noun to an adjective.

Examples

In the following examples, 很 (hěn) is just a link (you could think of it as a substitute for the verb "to be"), and the sentences could be translated as "(Noun) is (adjective)."

* 我 很 好。
  Wǒ hěn hǎo.
  I'm good.

▷ 你 很 漂亮。
  Nǐ hěn piàoliang.
  You are pretty.

▷ 他 很 高兴。
  Tā hěn gāoxìng.
  He is happy.

▷ 中文 很 难。
  Zhōngwén hěn nán.
  Chinese is difficult.

---

1. Connecting nouns with "shi" (A1), page 53

* 老板 很 生气。

  Lǎobǎn hěn shēngqì.

  The boss is angry.

* 我们 很 累。

  Wǒmen hěn lèi.

  We're tired.

* 我哥哥也 很 高。

  Wǒ gēge yě hěn gāo.

  My older brother is also tall.

* 你家也 很 远吗?

  Nǐ jiā yě hěn yuǎn ma?

  Is your house also far away?

* 爸爸 很 忙，妈妈也很忙。

  Bàba hěn máng, māma yě hěn máng.

  Dad is busy, and mom is also busy.

* 他和他弟弟都 很 帅。

  Tā hé tā dìdi dōu hěn shuài.

  He and his younger brother are both handsome.

Remember that 是 **(shì) is not used to link adjectives to nouns**. This is a classic mistake that almost everyone makes when learning Chinese. Make sure you use 很 (hěn) and not 是 (shì) to link adjectives to nouns, as shown below:

✖ 他 是 高。

  Tā shì gāo.

✔ 他 很 高。

  Tā hěn gāo.

  He is tall.

What 很 (hěn) Really Means

If you're like most learners, when you first learn this pattern, you're thinking, *"How can 很 (hěn) mean "very" one minute, but then nothing but a "link" the next? How do I know if anything means anything in this language?"* That's a reasonable response. But in the case of these "Noun + Adj." sentences, you just have to think of this usage of 很 (hěn) as an exception. It's just part of the structure.

If you actually want to add the meaning of "very" into the sentence, you could use another adverb instead of 很 (hěn). One good choice is 非常 (fēicháng).

✔ 他 非常 高。

Tā fēicháng gāo.

He is very tall.

Similar to

- Age with "sui"
- Connecting nouns with "shi" (A1), page 53
- The "also" adverb "ye" (A1), page 19
- Expressing "both A and B" with "you"
- Special verbs with "hen"
- Superlative "zui"
- Adjectives with "name" and "zheme"
- Reduplication of adjectives

Tag questions with "ma" (A1)

As well as yes/no questions, you can also form tag questions with 吗 (ma). Tag questions are quick questions that are tagged on the end of a sentence to ask for confirmation. In English, this is often done with "right?" or negatively with "isn't it?"

The easiest way to do this in Chinese is to add some kind of confirmation word and 吗 (ma) on the end of the sentence.

Structure

As you can see below, the pattern typically involves words like 好 (hǎo), 对 (duì), 是 (shì), or 可以 (kěyǐ), followed by 吗 (ma).

······, 好 / 对 / 是 / 可以 + 吗?

By placing these on the end of a sentence, you can soften a suggestion or request confirmation.

Examples

▷ 这样做，对吗 ?
Zhèyàng zuò, duì ma ?
Do it like this, right?

• 你们见过，对吗 ?
Nǐmen jiàn guo, duì ma ?
You've met, right?

▷ 他们昨天都没去，是吗 ?
Tāmen zuótiān dōu méi qù, shì ma ?
They didn't go yesterday, right?

• 你没来过，是吗 ?
Nǐ méi lái guo, shì ma ?
You haven't been here, right?

• 你喜欢我妹妹，是吗 ?
Nǐ xǐhuan wǒ mèimei, shì ma ?
You like my younger sister, huh?

* 我们去你家，好吗？

  Wǒmen qù nǐ jiā, hǎo ma ?

  Let's go to your place, OK?

* 不要告诉他，好吗？

  Bùyào gàosu tā, hǎo ma ?

  Don't tell him, OK?

* 今天我们都不喝酒，好吗？

  Jīntiān wǒmen dōu bù hējiǔ, hǎo ma ?

  Let's all not drink alcohol today, OK?

* 我现在想去洗手间，可以吗？

  Wǒ xiànzài xiǎng qù xǐshǒujiān, kěyǐ ma ?

  I want to go to the bathroom now. Is that OK?

* 妈妈，我要吃巧克力，可以吗？

  Māma, wǒ yào chī qiǎokèlì, kěyǐ ma ?

  Mom, I want to eat chocolate. May I?

Similar to

* Questions with "ne" (A1), page 29

* Tag questions with "bu"

* Yes-no questions with "ma"

* Advanced yes-no questions with "ma"

Questions with "ne" (A1)

The particle 呢 (ne) can be used to ask reciprocal questions, also known as "bounce back" questions. 呢 (ne) can also be used to form simple questions asking "what about...?" or "how about...?"

General Questions with 呢 (ne)

Structure

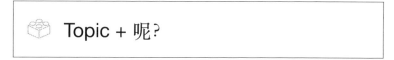

And it's as simple as that. Say what you want to ask about, then stick 呢 (ne) on the end. A very common way to use this is to return a question after being asked it. The classic example is this exchange:

A: 你好吗?

Nǐ hǎo ma?

B: 我很好。你 呢 ?

Wǒ hěn hǎo. Nǐ ne ?

A: 我也很好。

Wǒ yě hěn hǎo.

Examples

More 呢 (ne) examples (each of these can be translated as a "what about" question):

这个很好，那个 呢 ?

Zhège hěn hǎo, nàge ne ?

This one is good. What about that one?

这个用中文怎么说? 那个 呢 ?

Zhège yòng Zhōngwén zěnme shuō? Nàge ne ?

How do I say this in Chinese? And that?

我在家，你 呢 ?

Wǒ zài jiā. Nǐ ne ?

I'm at home. What about you?

- 你爸爸是上海人，你妈妈 呢 ?

  Nǐ bàba shì Shànghǎi rén, nǐ māma ne ?

  Your father is Shanghainese. And your mom?

- 你哥哥有工作，弟弟 呢 ?

  Nǐ gēge yǒu gōngzuò. Dìdi ne ?

  Your big brother has a job. What about your little brother?

- 北京下雨了。上海 呢 ?

  Běijīng xiàyǔ le. Shànghǎi ne ?

  It's raining in Beijing. How about in Shanghai?

- 我现在要出去。你 呢 ?

  Wǒ xiànzài yào chūqù. Nǐ ne ?

  I'm going to go out now. How about you?

▷ 我知道你会说中文。你老公 呢 ?

  Wǒ zhīdào nǐ huì shuō Zhōngwén. Nǐ lǎogōng ne ?

  I know you can speak Chinese. What about your husband?

- 这个周末我想去酒吧。你们 呢 ?

  Zhège zhōumò wǒ xiǎng qù jiǔbā. Nǐmen ne ?

  I want to go to a bar this weekend. What about you all?

- 今天晚上没空？明天晚上 呢 ?

  Jīntiān wǎnshang méi kòng? Míngtiān wǎnshang ne ?

  You don't have time tonight? What about tomorrow evening?

Asking "Where" with 呢 (ne)

You'll occasionally hear someone seemingly using 呢 (ne) out of the blue. When this happens, they're usually asking *where* someone or something is, and they expect that you know what they're talking about and know where that person or thing is.

Structure

 [Missing Person / Thing] + 呢?

Examples

This one is simple, so just a few examples are needed:

- 钱 呢 ?

  Qián ne ?

  Where's the money?

- 你妈妈 呢 ?

  Nǐ māma ne ?

  Where's your mom?

- 我的手机 呢 ?

  Wǒ de shǒujī ne ?

  Where's my cell phone?

Similar to

- Tag questions with "ma" (A1), page 27
- Yes-no questions with "ma"
- Sentence-final interjection "a"
- Advanced yes-no questions with "ma"
- Softening the tone of questions with "ne"

Placement of question words (A1)

Who, *what*, *when*, *where*, *why*, and *how*: these question words are all used when forming questions in Chinese. The important thing to remember is that word order is the same in Chinese for questions and statements.

Overview
Common Question Words List

In English, question words are also known as *wh-words*, as the majority of them begin with *wh*:

- 什么

  shénme

  what

- 哪里、哪儿

  nǎlǐ, nǎr

  where

- 哪个

  nǎge

  which

- 谁

  shéi

  who

  In spoken Chinese, people normally say "shéi," not "shuí"

- 什么时候

  shénme shíhou

  when

- 为什么

  wèishénme

  why

- 怎么

  zěnme

  how

- 多少

  duōshao

  how many / how much

Rules

In English, question words have to be placed at the beginning of the sentence. This involves changing the word order to allow this rearrangement. In Chinese, using question words is a lot simpler. You simply place a question word in the place of the thing you want to ask about. *Nothing needs to be rearranged.*

So if the statement is

* 我是 小李 。

  Wǒ shì Xiǎo Lǐ .

  I am Xiao Li.

the question form - "who are you?" - has the same word order:

* 你是 谁 ?

  Nǐ shì shéi ?

  Who are you? (you are who?)

This works for whatever it is you want to ask about. The question form has the same word order as the statement form.

Expressing "What" with 什么 (shénme)

Structure

> Subj. + Verb + 什么 + (Noun) ?

Examples

A: 这是 什么 ?

Zhè shì shénme ?

What is this?

B: 这是 我的 iPad 。

Zhè shì wǒ de iPad .

This is my iPad.

A: 你喜欢吃 什么 菜?

Nǐ xǐhuan chī shénme cài?

What kind of food do you like?

B: 我喜欢吃 中国菜 。

Wǒ xǐhuan chī Zhōngguó cài .

I like Chinese food.

A: 你用 什么 手机?

Nǐ yòng shénme shǒujī?

What kind of cell phone do you use?

B: 我用 iPhone 。

Wǒ yòng iPhone .

I use an iPhone.

A: 你在看 什么 书?

Nǐ zài kàn shénme shū?

What kind of book are you reading?

B: 我在看 小说 。

Wǒ zài kàn xiǎoshuō .

I am reading a novel.

A: 他开 什么 车?

Tā kāi shénme chē?

What kind of car does he drive?

B: 他开 宝马 。

Tā kāi Bǎomǎ .

He drives a BMW.

Expressing "Where" with 哪里 (nǎlǐ) / 哪儿 (nǎr)

The words 哪里 (nǎlǐ) and 哪儿 (nǎr) mean the same thing. The difference is simply regional preference: 哪里 (nǎlǐ) is preferred in the south (Shanghai, Taiwan), whereas 哪儿 (nǎr) is preferred in the north (Beijing, Xi'an).

Structure

 Subj. + Verb + 哪里 / 哪儿 ?

Examples

A: 你在 哪里 ?

Nǐ zài nǎlǐ ?

Where are you?

B: 我在 家 。

Wǒ zài jiā .

I'm at home.

A: 你要去 哪儿 ?

Nǐ yào qù nǎr ?

Where are you going now?

B: 我要去 洗手间 。

Wǒ yào qù xǐshǒujiān .

I'm going to the bathroom.

A: 我们在 哪儿 ?

Wǒmen zài nǎr ?

Where are we?

B: 我们在 南京西路 。

Wǒmen zài Nánjīng Xī Lù .

We are at West Nanjing road.

A: 这个周末你想去 哪儿 ?

Zhège zhōumò nǐ xiǎng qù nǎr ?

Where do you want to go this weekend?

B: 我想去 公园 。

Wǒ xiǎng qù gōngyuán .

I want to go to the park.

A: 你好，你要去 哪儿 ?

Nǐhǎo, nǐ yào qù nǎr ?

Hello, where do you want to go?

B: 我要去 外滩 。

Wǒ yào qù Wàitān .

I want to go to the Bund.

Expressing "Which" with 哪个 (nǎge)

Structure

 Subj. + Verb + 哪个 (+ Noun) ?

Examples

A: 你要 哪个 ?

Nǐ yào nǎge ?

Which one do you want?

B: 我要 这个 。

Wǒ yào zhège .

I want this one.

A: 你喜欢 哪个菜 ?

Nǐ xǐhuan nǎge cài ?

Which dish do you like?

B: 我喜欢 这个菜 。

Wǒ xǐhuan zhège cài .

I like this dish.

A: 我们去 哪个饭店 ?

Wǒmen qù nǎge fàndiàn ?

Which restaurant are we going to?

B: 我们去 你妈妈的饭店 。

Wǒmen qù nǐ māma de fàndiàn .

We are going to your mom's restaurant.

A: 你在 哪个房间 ?

Nǐ zài nǎge fángjiān ?

Which room are you in?

B: 我在 你的房间 。

Wǒ zài nǐ de fángjiān .

I'm in your room.

A: 你住在 哪个区 ?

Nǐ zhù zài nǎge qū ?

Which district do you live in?

B: 我住在 静安区 。

Wǒ zhù zài Jìng'ān Qū .

I live in Jing'an District.

Expressing "Who" with 谁 (shéi)

Structure

Subj. + 是 + 谁 ?

谁 + Verb ?

Examples

A: 你是 谁 ?

Nǐ shì shéi ?

Who are you?

B: 我是 他女朋友 。

Wǒ shì tā nǚpéngyou .

I'm his girlfriend.

A: 她是 谁 ?

Tā shì shéi ?

Who is she?

B: 她是 我的老师 。

Tā shì wǒ de lǎoshī .

She's my teacher.

A: 你不喜欢 谁 ?

Nǐ bù xǐhuan shéi ?

Who do you not like?

B: 我不喜欢 我的老板 。

Wǒ bù xǐhuan wǒ de lǎobǎn .

I don't like my boss.

A: 谁 想去?

Shéi xiǎng qù?

Who wants to go?

B: 我 想去。

Wǒ xiǎng qù.

I want to go.

A: 谁 想喝咖啡?

Shéi xiǎng hē kāfēi?

Who wants to drink coffee?

B: 我 想喝咖啡。

Wǒ xiǎng hē kāfēi.

I want to drink coffee.

Expressing "When" with 什么时候 (shénme shíhou)
Structure

 Subj. + 什么时候 + Predicate ?

Examples for asking and telling *when* (to keep things simple, we'll just include questions about the future; asking questions about the past can be slightly more complicated and may involve the "shi... de" construction).

Examples

A: 你 什么时候 来?

Nǐ shénme shíhou lái?

When are you coming?

B: 我 明天 来。

Wǒ míngtiān lái.

I'm coming tomorrow.

A: 你们 什么时候 走?
Nǐmen shénme shíhou zǒu?
When are you guys leaving?

B: 我们 下个月 走。
Wǒmen xià gè yuè zǒu.
We're leaving next month.

A: 我们 什么时候 吃饭?
Wǒmen shénme shíhou chīfàn?
When are we eating?

B: 我们 6 点 吃饭。
Wǒmen liù diǎn chīfàn.
We're eating at 6:00.

A: 爸爸 什么时候 回来?
Bàba shénme shíhou huílái?
When is dad coming back?

B: 爸爸 周末 回来。
Bàba zhōumò huílái.
Dad is coming back this weekend.

A: 你的飞机 什么时候 到上海?
Nǐ de fēijī shénme shíhou dào Shànghǎi?
When is your airplane arriving in Shanghai?

B: 晚上八点 。
Wǎnshang bā diǎn.
Eight o'clock this evening.

Expressing "Why" with 为什么 (wèishénme)
Structure

 Subj. + 为什么 + Predicate ?

Examples

A: 你 为什么 学中文?
Nǐ wèishénme xué Zhōngwén?
Why do you study Chinese?

B: 因为 我在中国工作。

Yīnwèi wǒ zài Zhōngguó gōngzuò.

Because I'm working in China.

A: 他们 为什么 不喝咖啡?

Tāmen wèishénme bù hē kāfēi?

Why don't you drink coffee?

B: 因为 咖啡很苦。

Yīnwèi kāfēi hěn kǔ.

Because coffee is bitter.

A: 他 为什么 不来?

Tā wèishénme bù lái?

Why isn't he coming?

B: 因为 他很忙。

Yīnwèi tā hěn máng.

Because he is busy.

A: 你早上 为什么 不在?

Nǐ zǎoshang wèishénme bù zài?

Why were you not here this morning?

B: 因为 我出去见朋友了。

Yīnwèi wǒ chūqù jiàn péngyou le.

Because I went out to meet some friends.

A: 这些外国人 为什么 不喜欢中国?

Zhèxiē wàiguó rén wèishénme bù xǐhuan Zhōngguó?

Why do these foreigners not like China?

B: 因为 中国人太多。

Yīnwèi Zhōngguó rén tài duō.

Because China has a lot of people.

Expressing "How" with 怎么 (zěnme)
Structure

 Subj. + 怎么 + Verb (+ Obj.) ?

Examples

A: 你 怎么 学习中文?

Nǐ zěnme xuéxí Zhōngwén?

How do you study Chinese?

B: 我 用 Grammar Wiki 学习中文。

Wǒ yòng Grammar Wiki xuéxí Zhōngwén.

I use the Grammar Wiki to study Chinese.

A: 你 怎么 上网?

Nǐ zěnme shàngwǎng?

How do you go online?

B: 我 用手机 上网。

Wǒ yòng shǒujī shàngwǎng.

I use my cell phone to go online.

A: 你 怎么 去北京?

Nǐ zěnme qù Běijīng?

How do you go to Beijing?

B: 我 坐火车 去。

Wǒ zuò huǒchē qù.

I take the train.

A: 你们 怎么 回家?

Nǐmen zěnme huíjiā?

How are you guys going to get home?

B: 我 开车 回家。

Wǒ kāichē huíjiā.

I'm driving home.

A: 你 怎么 买票?

Nǐ zěnme mǎi piào?

How do you buy tickets?

B: 我 上网 买票。

Wǒ shàngwǎng mǎi piào.

I go online to buy tickets.

Similar to

- Basic sentence order (A1), page 12

- How to do something with "zenme"

- Asking why with "zenme"

Expressing possession with "de" (A1)

In Chinese, possession is marked with the particle 的 (de), placed after the "owner" noun or noun phrase. This particle works in a similar way to apostrophe-"s" in English, but is used much more broadly in Chinese. This article highlights one of its simplest and most common usages.

Structure

Noun 1 + 的 + Noun 2

This means "**Noun 1's Noun 2**" (where Noun 2 belongs to Noun 1).

The structure is super simple. It will take a bit of time before you realize how truly universal this pattern is. It doesn't matter whether the "Noun 1" is a person, place, or thing, or even if it's a pronoun (like "he," "she," or "it"). The structure stays consistent.

Examples

- 我 的 老师
  wǒ de lǎoshī
  my teacher

- 你 的 手机
  nǐ de shǒujī
  your cell phone

- 我们 的 钱
  wǒmen de qián
  our money

- 他们 的 东西
  tāmen de dōngxi
  their stuff

- 爸爸 的 车
  bàba de chē
  dad's car

- 你们 的 菜

  nǐmen de cài

  your food

- 北京 的 空气

  Běijīng de kōngqì

  Beijing's air

- 公司 的 老板

  gōngsī de lǎobǎn

  the company's boss

- 上海 的 天气

  Shànghǎi de tiānqì

  Shanghai's weather

- 老师 的 朋友

  lǎoshī de péngyou

  teacher's friend

Similar to

- Expressing close possession without "de"
- Expressing possession with "you" (A1), page 45

Expressing possession with "you" (A1)

有 (yǒu) can be used in various ways, but the most basic meaning of this verb you need to know is "to have."

Structure

 Subj. + 有 + Obj.

Examples

- 我 有 钱。
  Wǒ yǒu qián.
  I have money.

- 你 有 房子吗?
  Nǐ yǒu fángzi ma?
  Do you have a house?

▷ 她没 有 车。
  Tā méi yǒu chē.
  She doesn't have a car.

- 他 有 女朋友吗?
  Tā yǒu nǚpéngyou ma?
  Does he have a girlfriend?

▷ 我们 有 三个女儿。
  Wǒmen yǒu sān gè nǚ'ér.
  We have three daughters.

- 我们家 有 两个公司。
  Wǒmen jiā yǒu liǎng gè gōngsī.
  Our family has two companies.

- 你 有 一百块钱吗?
  Nǐ yǒu yī bǎi kuài qián ma?
  Do you have 100 kuài RMB?

- 你的老师 有 iPad 吗?

  Nǐ de lǎoshī yǒu iPad ma?

  Does your teacher have an iPad?

- 我爸爸没 有 工作。

  Wǒ bàba méi yǒu gōngzuò.

  My dad doesn't have a job.

- 今天你 有 课吗?

  Jīntiān nǐ yǒu kè ma?

  Do you have classes today?

Negating 有 (yǒu)

The verb 有 (yǒu) is negated in a special way. Unlike most verbs, it is negated with 没 (méi) instead of 不 (bù). The negative form of 有 (yǒu) then, is 没有 (méiyǒu). For more on that topic, see our article on negation of "you" with "mei."[1]

Similar to

- Expressing existence with "you" (A1), page 58

Standard negation with "bu" (A1)

不 (bù) is generally used to negate a verb in the present or future, or to talk about what you do not do, as a habit. So expressing things like "I don't want to go" or "I'm not going" or "I don't eat meat" would be typical uses of 不 (bù).

Negating Verbs

Structure

The standard way to negate verbs in Chinese is with 不 (bù). To negate a verb, simply place 不 (bù) before it:

 Subj. + 不 + Verb + Obj.

Examples

* 他们 不 是 坏孩子。

  Tāmen bù shì huài háizi.

  They are not bad kids.

* 我们 不 喝 酒。

  Wǒmen bù hē jiǔ.

  We don't drink alcohol.

* 我今天 不 想工作 。

  Wǒ jīntiān bù xiǎng gōngzuò .

  I don't want to work today.

* 你 不 喜欢 我吗?

  Nǐ bù xǐhuan wǒ ma?

  Do you not like me?

* 为什么你 不 喜欢喝 咖啡?

  Wèishénme nǐ bù xǐhuan hē kāfēi?

  Why don't you like to drink coffee?

Almost all verbs can be negated with 不 (bù) (unless you're talking about the past). The only verb that can never be negated with 不 (bù) is <u>有 (yǒu)</u>[1].

---

1. Negation of "you" with "mei" (A1), page 50

✗ 我 不 有 时间。

Wǒ bù yǒu shíjiān.

✔ 我 没 有 时间。

Wǒ méi yǒu shíjiān.

I don't have time.

Negating Adjectives

As it turns out, the structure with an adjective is basically the same as the one with a verb.

Structure

Subj. + 不 + Adj.

Examples

- 我 不 饿 。

  Wǒ bù è.

  I'm not hungry.

- 这个 不 贵 。

  Zhège bù guì.

  This is not expensive.

- 公司 不 大 。

  Gōngsī bù dà.

  The company is not big.

- 老板今天很 不 高兴 。

  Lǎobǎn jīntiān hěn bù gāoxìng.

  The boss is very unhappy today.

- 我哥哥 不 高 ，但是很帅。

  Wǒ gēge bù gāo, dànshì hěn shuài.

  My older brother is not tall, but he is very handsome.

Similar to

- Connecting nouns with "shi" (A1), page 53
- Negation of "you" with "mei" (A1), page 50
- Negation of past actions with "meiyou"
- Comparing "bu" and "mei"

Negation of "you" with "mei" (A1)

The verb 有 (yǒu) is negated differently from ordinary verbs. Rather than placing 不 (bù) before it as with other verbs, you must use 没 (méi) to negate the verb 有 (yǒu).

Structure

Nearly all verbs can be negated with 不 (bù)₁. The verb 有 (yǒu) is an important exception to this rule, and must be negated with 没 (méi).

> 没 + 有 (+ Obj.)

Note: because of the special relationship between 没 (méi) and 有 (yǒu), the pinyin for 没有 is normally written without a space: "méiyǒu."

Examples

- 我 没有 问题。

  Wǒ méiyǒu wèntí.

  I don't have any questions.

- 我们现在 没有 钱。

  Wǒmen xiànzài méiyǒu qián.

  We don't have money now.

- 他 没有 工作吗?

  Tā méiyǒu gōngzuò ma?

  Does he not have a job?

- 他们 没有 爸爸妈妈。

  Tāmen méiyǒu bàba māma.

  They don't have parents.

- 我们在北京 没有 房子。

  Wǒmen zài Běijīng méiyǒu fángzi.

  We don't have a house in Beijing.

---

1. Standard negation with "bu" (A1), page 47

* 你爸爸 没有 手机吗?

  Nǐ bàba méiyǒu shǒujī ma?

  Does your dad not have a cell phone?

* 你们在上海 没有 朋友吗?

  Nǐmen zài Shànghǎi méiyǒu péngyou ma?

  Do you not have friends in Shanghai?

* 我的老师现在 没有 男朋友。

  Wǒ de lǎoshī xiànzài méiyǒu nánpéngyou.

  My teacher doesn't have a boyfriend now.

* 他们都 没有 电脑吗?

  Tāmen dōu méiyǒu diànnǎo ma?

  Do they all not have computers?

* 这个周末你们都 没有 时间吗?

  Zhège zhōumò nǐmen dōu méiyǒu shíjiān ma?

  Do you all not have time this weekend?

Remember that trying to negate 有 (yǒu) with 不 (bù) is a classic mistake that many people make in the early stages of studying Chinese:

* ✗ 我 不 有 车。

  Wǒ bù yǒu chē.

  Never use 不 with 有!

* ✔ 我 没 有 车。

  Wǒ méi yǒu chē.

  I don't have a car.

  Always use 没 with 有.

Never use 不 (bù) with 有 (yǒu).

The Short Form of 没有 (méiyǒu) is 没 (méi)

没有 (méiyǒu) can be shortened to 没 (méi) without altering its meaning.

* 我 没 钱。

  Wǒ méi qián.

  I don't have money.

* 你 没 男朋友吗?

  Nǐ méi nánpéngyou ma?

  Do you not have a boyfriend?

* 你们 没 车吗?

  Nǐmen méi chē ma?

  You don't have a car?

* 老板现在 没 时间。

  Lǎobǎn xiànzài méi shíjiān.

  The boss doesn't have time right now.

* 我 没 工作，我老公也 没 工作。

  Wǒ méi gōngzuò, wǒ lǎogōng yě méi gōngzuò.

  I don't have a job. My husband doesn't have a job either.

Similar to

- Expressing existence with "you" (A1), page 58

- Expressing possession with "you" (A1), page 45

- Negation of past actions with "meiyou"

- Standard negation with "bu" (A1), page 47

- Basic comparisons with "meiyou"

- Comparing "bu" and "mei"

Connecting nouns with "shi" (A1)

The verb *to be* is not used in Chinese the same way as it is in English. In Chinese, 是 (shì) is for connecting nouns, and is generally not used with adjectives.

Basic Usage

Structure

The structure for connecting nouns with 是 (shì) is:

Noun 1 + 是 + Noun 2

This is equivalent to "Noun 1 **is** Noun 2" in English.

Chinese does not conjugate verbs. That is, the form of the verb is the same no matter who is doing it. In this case, it is always 是 (shì) and never changes. As you can see, it's easy to form simple sentences expressing *to be* in Chinese. The only tricky thing about 是 (shì) in Chinese is that it's used to link *two nouns*, so you can't rely too much on translating directly from English when it comes to expressing the English verb "to be" in Chinese.

Examples

* 我 是 学生。

  Wǒ shì xuésheng.

  I am a student.

* 你 是 John 吗?

  Nǐ shì John ma?

  Are you John?

* 他们 是 有钱人。

  Tāmen shì yǒuqián rén.

  They are rich people.

* 你 是 老板吗?

  Nǐ shì lǎobǎn ma?

  Are you the boss?

- 这 是 我男朋友。

  Zhè shì wǒ nánpéngyou.

  This is my boyfriend.

- 那 是 你们公司吗?

  Nà shì nǐmen gōngsī ma?

  Is that your company?

- 你妈妈 是 老师吗?

  Nǐ māma shì lǎoshī ma?

  Is your mother a teacher?

- 这都 是 你的钱。

  Zhè dōu shì nǐ de qián.

  This is all your money.

- 那 是 什么菜?

  Nà shì shénme cài?

  What food is that?

- 我也 是 他的朋友。

  Wǒ yě shì tā de péngyou.

  I am also his friend.

Other Uses of 是 (shì)

Be careful and take note. As you can see above, 是 (shì) is only used to link two nouns. It can't be used to link a noun and an adjective. This is a very common mistake for people just beginning to learn Chinese. For that kind of sentence, you'll want to use a different structure with <u>the linking word 很 (hěn)</u>[1].

In Chinese it is also possible to use the phrase "是不是 (shì bu shì)?" It can be used at the beginning or end of a sentence. It's meaning is quite similar to the English expressions "right" and "aren't you?" This is very useful if you want to express concern for a person, or if you want to mix up your sentence structure a bit and make it more interesting. The 是不是 (shì bu shì) pattern is also part of affirmative-negative questions.

Another way to use 是 (shì) is to <u>use it as a tag question</u>[2]. You can add "是吗?" (shì ma?) to the end of a question to mean the English equivalent of: "is it" or "yeah?" Using this in a question usually allows the speaker to get a confirmation answer.

---

1. Simple "noun + adjective" sentences (A1), page 24
2. Tag questions with "ma" (A1), page 27

Examples

- 他没听到，是不是？

  Tā méi tīngdào, shì bu shì ?

  He didn't hear you, right?

- 你 是不是 还没吃饭？

  Nǐ shì bu shì hái méi chīfàn?

  Haven't you eaten yet?

- 你们 是不是 中国人？

  Nǐmen shì bu shì Zhōngguó rén?

  Are you Chinese?

- 你到了，是吗？

  Nǐ dào le, shì ma ?

  You have arrived, yeah?

- 你有两个孩子，是吗？

  Nǐ yǒu liǎng gè háizi, shì ma ?

  You have two kids, yeah?

Similar to

- Simple "noun + adjective" sentences (A1), page 24
- Standard negation with "bu" (A1), page 47

Expressing existence in a place with "zai" (A1)

The verb 在 (zài) expresses existence in a location, similar to how we say in English, "to be at" or "to be in."

Structure

The verb 在 (zài) is used to express existence in a place. English does not have a verb exclusively for this purpose, and instead uses "to be" with a preposition. In Chinese, 在 (zài) can cover both of these roles.

Subj. + 在 + Place

Remember that you don't need another verb in this construction. It can be tempting to try use 是 (shì), as English uses "to be," but this is not correct. 在 (zài) is the only verb needed.

Examples

* 我 在 上海。

  Wǒ zài Shànghǎi.

  I'm in Shanghai.

* 他们 在 英国。

  Tāmen zài Yīngguó.

  They're in England.

* 老板 在 外面。

  Lǎobǎn zài wàimiàn.

  The boss is outside.

* 他不 在 学校。

  Tā bù zài xuéxiào.

  He's not at school.

* 她现在 在 家吗?

  Tā xiànzài zài jiā ma?

  Is she at home now?

* 你 在 公司吗?

  Nǐ zài gōngsī ma?

  Are you at the office?

  Literally, "Are you at the company?"

- 老师不 在 办公室吗？

  Lǎoshī bù zài bàngōngshì ma?

  Is the teacher not in the office?

- 谁 在 楼上？

  Shéi zài lóushàng?

  Who is upstairs?

- 我和朋友 在 酒吧。

  Wǒ hé péngyou zài jiǔbā.

  I'm with a friend at a bar.

- 你们明天 在 北京吗？

  Nǐmen míngtiān zài Běijīng ma?

  Are you guys in Beijing tomorrow?

Similar to

- Expressing location with "zai… shang / xia / li"

- Indicating location with "zai" before verbs (A2), page 17

- Special cases of "zai" following verbs

- Idiomatic phrases with "zai"

Expressing existence with "you" (A1)

The verb 有 (yǒu), which means "to have," can also be used to express existence. This is similar to saying "there is" or "there are" in English.

Structure

Literally, this structure expresses that a place "has" a thing, which is to say, that thing is in the place.

 Place + 有 + Obj.

Examples

* 我家 有 很多小狗。

  Wǒ jiā yǒu hěn duō xiǎo gǒu.

  There are a lot of puppies in my home.

* 我们学校 有 很多帅哥。

  Wǒmen xuéxiào yǒu hěn duō shuàigē.

  There are a lot of cute guys in our school.

* 日本 有 很多中国人。

  Rìběn yǒu hěn duō Zhōngguó rén.

  There are many Chinese people in Japan.

* 这个酒吧 有 很多美女。

  Zhège jiǔbā yǒu hěn duō měinǚ.

  There are a lot of pretty girls in this bar.

* 你家 有 牛奶吗?

  Nǐ jiā yǒu niúnǎi ma?

  Is there milk in your house?

* 这里 有 一个问题。

  Zhèlǐ yǒu yī gè wèntí.

  There is a problem here.

- 房间里 有 人吗?

  Fángjiān lǐ yǒu rén ma?

  Is there anyone in the room?

- 杯子里 有 水吗?

  Bēizi lǐ yǒu shuǐ ma?

  Is there any water in the cup?

- 我的手机里 有 你的号码。

  Wǒ de shǒujī lǐ yǒu nǐ de hàomǎ.

  Your number is in my cell phone.

- 现在办公室里 有 人吗?

  Xiànzài bàngōngshì lǐ yǒu rén ma?

  Is there anyone in the office now?

Similar to

- Expressing possession with "you" (A1), page 45
- Negation of "you" with "mei" (A1), page 50

Using the verb "jiao" (A1)

The verb 叫 (jiào) is used to indicate what someone or something is called, or what someone or something's name is. Its usage can seem a little weird to beginners, so it gets its own grammar point.

Structure

The verb 叫 (jiào) means both "to call" and "to be called." It's an easy way to give names, using the following structure:

Subj. + 叫 + [Name]

This can be used to give your full name or just your first name.

Examples

- 我 叫 Tom。

  Wǒ jiào Tom.

  My name is Tom.

  Note: it even works if you don't have a Chinese name!

- 他 叫 李小龙。

  Tā jiào Lǐ Xiǎolóng.

  His name is Li Xiaolong.

  Note: this is the real name of Bruce Lee

- 我哥哥 叫 老马。

  Wǒ gēge jiào Lǎo Mǎ.

  My brother is called Lao Ma.

  Note: this is probably not his real name

- 那个 叫 什么?

  Nàge jiào shénme?

  What is that called?

- 这个美女 叫 Alana。

  Zhège měinǚ jiào Alana.

  This pretty girl is named Alana.

- 我们的老板 叫 John。

  Wǒmen de lǎobǎn jiào John.

  Our boss is named John.

- 我的狗 叫 Max。

  Wǒ de gǒu jiào Max.

  My dog is called Max.

- 这种手机 叫 iPhone。

  Zhè zhǒng shǒujī jiào iPhone.

  This kind of cell phone is called an iPhone.

- 你爸爸 叫 什么?

  Nǐ bàba jiào shénme?

  What is your dad's name?

- 这个地方 叫 外滩。

  Zhège dìfang jiào Wàitān.

  This place is called the Bund.

You can also ask people their names using 叫 (jiào):

- 你 叫 什么名字?

  Nǐ jiào shénme míngzi?

  What's your name?

Similar to

- Using the verb "xing"
- Causative verbs

Using the verb "qu" (A1)

You can use 去 (qù) whenever you have somewhere to go. It's pretty easy to get a handle on this verb; the only trick is getting used to not needing a word for "to" before the destination.

去 (qù) with Just a Place

The verb 去 (qù) means "to go," and is an easy way to talk about going to places.

Structure

> Subj. + 去 + [Place]

Notice that you don't need a word to express "to."

Examples

- 我 去 公司。

  Wǒ qù gōngsī.

  I'm going to the office.

  公司 literally means "company" but is often used to mean "office."

- 你 去 洗手间吗?

  Nǐ qù xǐshǒujiān ma?

  Are you going to the restroom?

- 下午我会 去 超市。

  Xiàwǔ wǒ huì qù chāoshì.

  In the afternoon, I'll go to the supermarket.

- 我们现在 去 公园。

  Wǒmen xiànzài qù gōngyuán.

  We're going to the park now.

- 晚上我们 去 酒吧。你去吗?

  Wǎnshang wǒmen qù jiǔbā. Nǐ qù ma?

  Tonight we're going to the bar. Are you going?

You can also use 去 (qù) for asking questions. (Note the use of question words and question particles.)

A: 你 去 哪儿 ?
Nǐ qù nǎr ?
Where are you going?

B: 我 去 学校 。
Wǒ qù xuéxiào .
I am going to school.

A: 你 去 我家 吗 ?
Nǐ qù wǒ jiā ma ?
Are you going to my place?

B: 我 去 。   *literally, "I'm going."*
Wǒ qù .
Yes.

When answering a yes-no question that uses 去 (qù) you don't need anything following it. However, it's important to note that you cannot just use 去 (qù) when there is no context.

去 (qù) with a Verb

Instead of a place, 去 (qù) can also be followed by some sort of action. The structure then means "go to do (something)," and "go and do (something)."

Structure

Examples

* 我 去 工作。
  Wǒ qù gōngzuò.
  I'm going to work.

* 他 去 上课。
  Tā qù shàngkè.
  He's going to class.

* 你想 去 旅行吗?

  Nǐ xiǎng qù lǚxíng ma?

  Would you like to go travel?

* 我们 去 吃饭吧。

  Wǒmen qù chīfàn ba.

  Let's go eat.

* 九点我们 去 买。

  Jiǔ diǎn wǒmen qù mǎi.

  At 9 o'clock, we'll go buy it.

Similar to

* Using "dao" to mean "to go to"

The "all" adverb "dou" (A1)

The adverb 都 (dōu) is used to express "all" in Chinese. It's common to use 都 (dōu) in a variety of sentences where it would seem unnecessary in English.

都 (dōu) for "All"

Structure

 Subj. + 都 + [Verb Phrase]

Remember that 都 (dōu) appears *after* the subject. A common mistake learners make is to put 都 (dōu) at the beginning of the sentence (as "all" often appears there in English). This isn't good Chinese - make sure you put 都 (dōu) after the subject and before the verb.

Examples

* 你们 都 认识 John 吗?

  Nǐmen dōu rènshi John ma?

  Do you all know John?

* 他们 都 在上海。

  Tāmen dōu zài Shànghǎi.

  They are all in Shanghai.

* 明天我们 都 可以去。

  Míngtiān wǒmen dōu kěyǐ qù.

  Tomorrow we all can go.

* 你们 都 用 wiki 吗?

  Nǐmen dōu yòng wiki ma?

  Do you all use the wiki?

* 我们 都 要冰水。

  Wǒmen dōu yào bīngshuǐ.

  We all want ice water.

都 (dōu) for "Both"

Chinese doesn't normally use a special word for "both" like English does. It just uses 都 (dōu) as if it were any other number greater than one. Chinese also doesn't have a special pattern like "neither / nor" for the negative case. Just use 都 (dōu) and make the sentence negative.

Structure

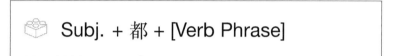

Subj. + 都 + [Verb Phrase]

This pattern should look familiar.

Examples

These examples follow exactly the same form in Chinese as the ones above. The only difference is that here we don't translate 都 (dōu) as "all" in English; we translate it as "both," and for negative cases, we translate it as "neither."

- 我们两个 都 爱你。

  Wǒmen liǎng gè dōu ài nǐ.

  The two of us both love you.

- 你爸爸和你妈妈 都 是美国人吗?

  Nǐ bàba hé nǐ māma dōu shì Měiguó rén ma?

  Are your father and your mother both Americans?

- 我和我太太 都 不吃肉。

  Wǒ hé wǒ tàitai dōu bù chī ròu.

  Neither my wife nor I eat meat.

- 你们两个 都 喜欢中国菜吗?

  Nǐmen liǎng gè dōu xǐhuan Zhōngguó cài ma?

  Do you both like Chinese food?

- 她和她老公 都 没有工作。

  Tā hé tā lǎogōng dōu méiyǒu gōngzuò.

  Neither she nor her husband has a job.

Similar to

- Emphasizing quantity with "dou"
- Using "ye" and "dou" together

Expressing "excessively" with "tai" (A1)

In Chinese, the simplest structure for expressing "too" in the sense of "excessively" is by using the word 太 (tài). Don't forget to also add 了 (le) after the adjective to keep your Chinese sounding natural.

Structure

太 + Adj. + 了

As in English, this can express that something really is excessive (often as a complaint), or can also colloquially express the meaning of "so" or "very."

Examples

The following examples sound a little bit like a complaint, or a reason for not doing something. They're similar to how we would use "too" in English, and the translations are straightforward.

- 米饭 太 多 了 。
  Mǐfàn tài duō le .
  There is too much rice.

- 现在 太 晚 了 。
  Xiànzài tài wǎn le .
  Now it's too late.

- 老板 太 忙 了 。
  Lǎobǎn tài máng le .
  The boss is too busy.

- 老师 太 累 了 。
  Lǎoshī tài lèi le .
  The teacher is too tired.

- 这个厕所 太 脏 了 。
  Zhège cèsuǒ tài zāng le .
  This restroom is too dirty.

In the following examples, the same exact pattern is used to exclaim how *good* something is, so these uses are totally *not* complaints. The English translations have to get a little more creative to express the same feeling in English.

* 你 太 好 了 。
  Nǐ tài hǎo le .
  You are so great.

* 他 太 帅 了 。
  Tā tài shuài le .
  He is very handsome.

* 这个女孩 太 漂亮 了 。
  Zhège nǚhái tài piàoliang le .
  This girl is so pretty.

* 小猫 太 可爱 了 ！
  Xiǎomāo tài kě'ài le !
  The kitten is so cute!

* 你的孩子 太 聪明 了 。
  Nǐ de háizi tài cōngming le .
  Your kids are wicked smart.

Note for the more advanced learner: This pattern can be used with modal verbs (e.g. 会 (huì), 能 (néng)) as well as psychological verbs (e.g. 喜欢 (xǐhuan), 想 (xiǎng), 爱 (ài)) to intensify the degree.

Source|Modern Mandarin Chinese Grammar: A Practical Guide|57) →buy

Similar to

- Expressing "a little too" with "you dian"

- Expressing "not very" with "bu tai"

- Expressing "really" with "zhen"

- Special verbs with "hen"

- Superlative "zui"

- Adjectives with "-ji le"

- Expressing "quite" with "ting"

- Expressing "a bit too"

Expressing "and" with "he" (A1)

When listing out multiple nouns, 和 (hé) is there to help you out. Just remember that 和 (hé) isn't a word you can use to translate just *any* usage of the English word "and."

Structure

The most common way to express "and" in Chinese is with 和 (hé). It's important to note that 和 (hé) **is mainly used to link nouns**. This is how you should use it *exclusively* as you get used to it. Don't try to link verbs (or whole sentences) with 和 (hé).

Noun 1 + 和 + Noun 2

Examples

* 你 和 我
  nǐ hé wǒ
  you and I

* 老板喜欢 咖啡 和 茶 。
  Lǎobǎn xǐhuan kāfēi hé chá .
  The boss likes coffee and tea.

* 我的爷爷 和 奶奶 都 70 岁。
  Wǒ de yéye hé nǎinai dōu qīshí suì.
  My grandpa and grandma are both 70 years old.

* 他 和 他女朋友 都喜欢中国菜。
  Tā hé tā nǚpéngyou dōu xǐhuan Zhōngguó cài.
  He and his girlfriend both like Chinese food.

* 你爸爸 和 你妈妈 都是美国人吗?
  Nǐ bàba hé nǐ māma dōu shì Měiguó rén ma?
  Are your father and your mother both Americans?

* 手机 和 电脑 都很贵。
  Shǒujī hé diànnǎo dōu hěn guì.
  Cell phones and computers are both expensive.

- 德语 和 法语 都很难吗?

  Déyǔ hé Fǎyǔ dōu hěn nán ma?

  Are both German and French difficult?

- 今天 和 明天 都可以吗?

  Jīntiān hé míngtiān dōu kěyǐ ma?

  Are today and tomorrow both OK?

(If you're unclear why the 都 (dōu) is used in the sentences above, see our article on the adverb 都 (dōu)[1].)

Just to be absolutely clear what we mean by using 和 (hé) with nouns only, here are two English examples of what you should and shouldn't try to express with 和 (hé):

⚠ I went to the store and bought some gum.

✔ I like to eat cucumbers and cheese.

Similar to

- Combining verbs with "bing"

- Expressing "and" with "he" (advanced)

---

1. The "all" adverb "dou" (A1), page 65

Offering choices with "haishi" (A1)

还是 (háishì) is used in Chinese to provide options in a **question**. This is equivalent to one of our uses of "or" in English.

Simplest Form

Structure

Option A + 还是 + Option B ?

When you're asked a question of this form, there are two ways you're expected to answer: either Option A or Option B. (Pick one, but not both.) It's not that no other answers are possible, it's that usually when you're asked a question this way, the person asking expects you to just choose one. For example, if asked if you'd like to drink coffee or tea, most people are going to choose one or the other, not ask for both. 还是 (háishì) is used to ask people to make that choice between the two.

Examples

- 我 还是 他 ?
  Wǒ háishì tā?
  Me or him?

- 一个 还是 两个 ?
  Yī gè háishì liǎng gè ?
  One or two?

- 辣的 还是 不辣的 ?
  Là de háishì bù là de ?
  Spicy or non-spicy?

- 冰的 还是 热的 ?
  Bīng de háishì rè de ?
  Cold or hot?

- 上海 还是 北京 ?
  Shànghǎi háishì Běijīng?
  Shanghai or Beijing?

The eternal China expat question!
Choose wisely...

Full Sentence Form

Structure

You can take the structure above, add a subject and a verb, and create all kinds of questions with the following structure:

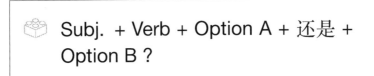

Subj. + Verb + Option A + 还是 + Option B ?

Examples

* 这是 水 还是 酒 ?

  Zhè shì shuǐ háishì jiǔ ?

  Is this water or alcohol?

* 他是 美国人 还是 英国人 ?

  Tā shì Měiguó rén háishì Yīngguó rén ?

  Is he American or British?

* 你喜欢 我 还是 我的钱 ?

  Nǐ xǐhuan wǒ háishì wǒ de qián ?

  Do you like me or my money?

* 你要喝 茶 还是 咖啡 ?

  Nǐ yào hē chá háishì kāfēi ?

  Do you want to drink tea or coffee?

* 你们想吃 中国菜 还是 法国菜 ?

  Nǐmen xiǎng chī Zhōngguó cài háishì Fǎguó cài ?

  Do you want to eat Chinese food or French food?

Please note that 还是 (háishì) is for offering options in a **question**. It should not be used for "or" in statements.

Similar to

- Affirmative-negative question

- Expressing "or" in statements

- Comparing "haishi" and "huozhe"

- Reviewing options with "ba"

Structure of numbers (A1)

Chinese handles numbers in a very consistent and logical way. Once you've mastered just a few tricky parts, you will know how to read out any number in Chinese.

One to One Hundred
Structure for the First Ten

You just have to memorize these ten; nothing tricky there.

Numeral	Character	Pinyin
1	一	yī
2	二	èr
3	三	sān
4	四	sì
5	五	wǔ
6	六	liù
7	七	qī
8	八	bā
9	九	jiǔ
10	十	shí

Phone Numbers

Like in American English, Chinese phone numbers are given as a string of individual numbers, using the digits 0-9. The only trick is that the number 1 is often pronounced "yāo" instead of "yī" to avoid confusion with number 7, which is pronounced "qī."

- 110   *Number for the police in the PRC*

  yāo yāo líng

- 120   *Number for an ambulance in the PRC*

  yāo èr líng

- 119   *Number to report a fire in the PRC*

  yāo yāo jiǔ

- 13501200120   *Cell phone numbers are 11 digits in the PRC*

yāo sān wǔ, líng yāo èr líng, líng yāo èr líng

Structure for Teens

Eleven, twelve and the teens are handled very logically. They're formed with 十 (shí) followed by a digit 一 (yī) to 九 (jiǔ). So eleven is 十一 (shíyī), twelve is 十二 (shí'èr), thirteen is 十三 (shísān), and so on up to nineteen, which is 十九 (shíjiǔ).

Numeral	Character	Pinyin
11	十一	shíyī
12	十二	shí'èr
13	十三	shísān
14	十四	shísì
15	十五	shíwǔ
16	十六	shíliù
17	十七	shíqī
18	十八	shíbā
19	十九	shíjiǔ

Structure for Tens

All the tens are also formed very logically. Twenty is 二十 (èrshí), thirty is 三十 (sānshí), and so on. Units in the tens are simply added on the end. So twenty one is 二十一 (èrshí-yī), thirty four is 三十四 (sānshí-sì), and ninety-nine is 九十九 (jiǔshí-jiǔ). All very logical and consistent.

Examples

Numeral	Character	Pinyin
20	二十	èrshí
23	二十三	èrshí-sān
30	三十	sānshí
39	三十九	sānshí-jiǔ
40	四十	sìshí
44	四十四	sìshí-sì
50	五十	wǔshí
73	七十三	qīshí-sān
82	八十二	bāshí-èr
97	九十七	jiǔshí-qī

And one hundred is simply 一百 (yībǎi), as in English. So you now know how to count to one hundred in Chinese.

After One Hundred
Dealing with Zeroes

Note: when there's a "0" in the middle of a number, you read it as 零 (líng), and don't put a unit (like "ten" or "hundred") after it. In the following examples, we'll show what happens when the "tens" place is a zero in a three-digit number.

Structure

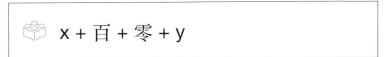

Examples

Numeral	Character	Pinyin
101	一百零一	yībǎi líng yī
202	二百零二	èrbǎi líng èr
206	二百零六	èrbǎi líng liù
305	三百零五	sānbǎi líng wǔ
407	四百零七	sìbǎi líng qī
504	五百零四	wǔbǎi líng sì
602	六百零二	liùbǎi líng èr
701	七百零一	qībǎi líng yī
803	八百零三	bābǎi líng sān
909	九百零九	jiǔbǎi líng jiǔ

For Numbers 110 and Greater

For numbers greater than 100, if the number ends in zero (110, 230, 370, 450, etc.), a number like 150 can be read as 一百五十 (yībǎi wǔshí), but is often read as 一百五 (yībǎi wǔ). In fact, reading it as 一百五 (yībǎi wǔ) *always* means 150, never 105. As described above, 105 would be read as 一百零五 (yībǎi líng wǔ).

For numbers greater than 100 that end in a number in the teens, it's normal to pronounce the ten as "yīshí" rather than just "shí" (see the examples below).

Also, sometimes the number "200" is read as 二百 (èrbǎi), but often it is read as 两百 (liǎngbǎi). Both are OK. (This is an 二 (èr) vs. 两 (liǎng) issue which you may or may not have encountered before.)

Structure

$$x + 百 + y + 十 + z$$

Examples

Numeral	Character	Pinyin
110	一百一十	yībǎi yīshí
111	一百一十一	yībǎi yīshí-yī
210	二百一十	èrbǎi yīshí
350	三百五十	sānbǎi wǔshí
480	四百八十	sìbǎi bāshí
550	五百五十	wǔbǎi wǔshí
635	六百三十五	liùbǎi sānshí-wǔ
777	七百七十七	qībǎi qīshí-qī
832	八百三十二	bābǎi sānshí-èr
999	九百九十九	jiǔbǎi jiǔshí-jiǔ

After One Thousand

千 (qiān) means "thousand" in Chinese. Its rules of usage are similar to the rules for "hundred." Just note that no matter how many zeroes are in the middle of the number, you just say 零 (líng) once.

Examples

Numeral	Character	Pinyin
1001	一千零一	yīqiān líng yī
1010	一千零一十	yīqiān líng yīshí
1019	一千零一十九	yīqiān líng yīshí-jiǔ
1020	一千零二十	yīqiān líng èrshí
1100	一千一百	yīqiān yībǎi
1101	一千一百零一	yīqiān yībǎi líng yī
1234	一千二百三十四	yīqiān èrbǎi sānshí-sì
2345	两千三百四十五	liǎngqiān sānbǎi sìshí-wǔ

8765	八千七百六十五	bāqiān qībǎi liùshí-wǔ
9999	九千九百九十九	jiǔqiān jiǔbǎi jiǔshí-jiǔ

10,000 and beyond

Things get a little trickier once you get to 10,000. If you're ready for it, you can move on to big numbers.

Similar to

- Comparing "er" and "liang"
- Structure of dates (A1), page 85
- Structure of days of the week (A1), page 82
- Structure of times (basic) (A1), page 79
- Approximating with sequential numbers
- Structure of times (advanced)

Structure of times (basic) (A1)

Time in Chinese, just like in English, is expressed by stating the hour first, and then the minute (big to small).

On the Hour

The time of day in Chinese is formed with a <u>number</u>[1] 1 to 12 (一 (yī) to 十二 (shí'èr)) followed by 点 (diǎn). This 点 (diǎn) is equivalent to *o'clock* in English. In China, people generally use a twelve-hour clock, preceded by 上午 (shàngwǔ) for "a.m." or 下午 (xiàwǔ) for "p.m." when necessary.

Structure

 (Date and/or time of day +) x 点

Sometimes people use the longer 点钟 (diǎnzhōng) instead of just 点 (diǎn), but you're fine using the short form.

Examples

If you want to include more specific information, start with the day or date, followed by the general time of day, with the exact clock time last. (This is the big-to-small pattern.) This is how Chinese gets around the need for "a.m." or "p.m.": use 上午 (shàngwǔ) for times in the morning, and 下午 (xiàwǔ) for times in the afternoon.

- 九 点
  jiǔ diǎn
  9 o'clock

- 上午七 点
  shàngwǔ qī diǎn
  7 o'clock a.m.

- 下午四 点
  xiàwǔ sì diǎn
  4 o'clock p.m.

- 中午十二 点
  zhōngwǔ shí'èr diǎn
  12 o'clock noon

---

1. Structure of numbers (A1), page 73

- 明天晚上七 点

  míngtiān wǎnshang qī diǎn

  7 o'clock p.m. tomorrow evening

- 9 月 9 号早上六 点

  jiǔ yuè jiǔ hào zǎoshang liù diǎn

  September 9th, 6 o'clock a.m.

- 星期三上午九 点

  Xīngqīsān shàngwǔ jiǔ diǎn

  Wednesday at 9 o'clock a.m.

Note that **two o'clock is 两点** (liǎng diǎn), not 二点 (èr diǎn). (For more information on when to use 两 (liǎng) vs. 二 (èr), see our article on comparing "er" and "liang").

"Twelve o'clock," however, is still 十二点 (shí'èr diǎn).

Half Hours

Half hours are added after 点 (diǎn) and are indicated with 半 (bàn).

Structure

$$\text{X 点} + \text{半}$$

Examples

- 五 点半

  wǔ diǎn bàn

  5:30

- 下午两 点半

  xiàwǔ liǎng diǎn bàn

  2:30 p.m.

- 星期天上午十 点半

  Xīngqītiān shàngwǔ shí diǎn bàn

  Sunday at 10:30 a.m.

- 昨天晚上七 点半

  zuótiān wǎnshang qī diǎn bàn

  7:30 yesterday evening

* 今天下午四 点半

jīntiān xiàwǔ sì diǎn bàn

4:30 p.m. this afternoon.

As a beginner, that should be all you need. If you've mastered all of these structures and want to get a little more advanced, see structure of times (advanced).

Similar to

- Structure of dates (A1), page 85
- Structure of numbers (A1), page 73
- Before a specific time with "yiqian"
- Structure of times (advanced)

Structure of days of the week (A1)

星期 (xīngqī) means "week" in Chinese. This is also used to indicate which weekday you are talking about.

Structure

Days of the week in Chinese are formed by the word "week" followed by a number:

English	Chinese
Monday	星期一 Xīngqīyī
Tuesday	星期二 Xīngqī'èr
Wednesday	星期三 Xīngqīsān
Thursday	星期四 Xīngqīsì
Friday	星期五 Xīngqīwǔ
Saturday	星期六 Xīngqīliù
Sunday	星期天 Xīngqītiān

Notice that Sunday is the only exception. Rather than a number, 天 (tiān) is used. More formally, Sunday is also referred to as 星期日 (Xīngqīrì).

One other implication of this system that you may not have noticed: "day one" is Monday. In Chinese culture, the first day of the week is Monday, and *not* Sunday.

Examples

* 今天是 星期一 吗?

    Jīntiān shì Xīngqīyī ma?

    Is today Monday?

    是 is optional

* 明天 星期五 ，太高兴了。

  Míngtiān Xīngqīwǔ , tài gāoxìng le.

  Tomorrow is Friday. I'm so happy.

  Optional 是 omitted

* 星期三 我不在上海。

  Xīngqīsān wǒ bù zài Shànghǎi.

  I'm not here in Shanghai on Wednesday.

* 星期二 早上我很忙。

  Xīngqī'èr zǎoshang wǒ hěn máng.

  I am busy on Tuesday morning.

* 你 星期天 要做什么？

  Nǐ Xīngqītiān yào zuò shénme?

  What are you doing on Sunday?

* 上个 星期五 我跟他见面了。

  Shàng gè Xīngqīwǔ wǒ gēn tā jiànmiàn le.

  I met him last Friday.

* 这个 星期三 晚上你有空吗？

  Zhège Xīngqīsān wǎnshang nǐ yǒu kòng ma?

  Are you free this Wednesday evening?

* 下个 星期四 是我的生日。

  Xià gè Xīngqīsì shì wǒ de shēngrì.

  My birthday is on next Thursday.

* 这个 星期五 晚上我们要去酒吧。

  Zhège Xīngqīwǔ wǎnshang wǒmen yào qù jiǔbā.

  We're going to a bar this Friday night.

* 星期六 和 星期天 我们不上班。

  Xīngqīliù hé Xīngqītiān wǒmen bù shàngbān.

  Saturday and Sunday we don't work.

Other Words for "Week"

Hopefully this doesn't freak you out, but there are actually two other ways to say "week" in Chinese. You should still learn 星期 (xīngqī) first, and that's really all you need as a beginner.

The other words for "week" are 礼拜 (lǐbài) and 周 (zhōu). Skip them for now unless you really need them.

Similar to

- Structure of dates (A1), page 85
- Structure of numbers (A1), page 73
- Structure of times (basic) (A1), page 79
- Structure of times (advanced)

Structure of dates (A1)

Dates in Chinese follow the order "year, month, day." This is in keeping with the "from big to small" trend which pervades many facets of Chinese culture.

Structure

Dates are arranged from largest unit to smallest: *year, month, day*.

> x 年 + y 月 + z 日

So April 1st, 2019 is **2019 年 4 月 1 日** (**èr-líng-yī-jiǔ** nián **Sìyuè yī** rì).

Note that 号 (hào) is commonly used in *spoken* Mandarin instead of 日 (rì):

> x 年 + y 月 + z 号

The above example becomes: **2019 年 4 月 1 号** (**èr-líng-yī-jiǔ** nián **Sìyuè yī** hào). In written Chinese, however, you will see 日 (rì) rather than 号 (hào).

Examples

- 1868 年 1 月 18 号
  Yī-bā-liù-bā nián Yī yuè shíbā hào
  January 18, 1868

- 1910 年 8 月 9 号
  Yī-jiǔ-yī-líng nián Bā yuè jiǔ hào
  August 9, 1910

- 2001 年 7 月 20 日
  èr-líng-líng-yī nián Qī yuè èrshí rì
  July 20th, 2001

- 1 月 1 日 是新年。
  Yī yuè yī rì shì Xīnnián.
  January 1st is New Year's Day.

- 12 月 24 日 是平安夜。

  Shí-èr yuè èrshí-sì rì shì Píng'ān Yè.

  December 24th is Christmas Eve.

- 10 月 1 号 我们去上海。

  Shí yuè yī hào wǒmen qù Shànghǎi.

  We will go to Shanghai on October 1st.

- 我 1990 年 7 月 出生。

  Wǒ Yī-jiǔ-jiǔ-líng nián Qī yuè chūshēng.

  I was born in July 1990.

- 你的生日是 11 月 11 号 吗?

  Nǐ de shēngrì shì Shíyī yuè shíyī hào ma?

  Is your birthday November 11th?

- 我 2006 年 4 月 17 号 认识了他。

  Wǒ èr-líng-líng-liù nián Sì yuè shíqī hào rènshi le tā.

  I met him on April 17, 2006.

- 1980 年 9 月 4 号 我们结婚了。

  Yī-jiǔ-bā-líng nián Jiǔ yuè sì hào wǒmen jiéhūn le.

  We got married on September 4th, 1980.

Similar to

- Structure of days of the week (A1), page 82

- Structure of numbers (A1), page 73

- Structure of times (basic) (A1), page 79

- Structure of times (advanced)

Measure word "ge" (A1)

个 (gè) is the most commonly used measure word. It can be used in a pinch for any noun if you can't think of a more precise measure word. (Although you might not sound quite as smart, you'll still get your point across). Also, for many nouns, 个 (gè) *is* the only correct measure word.

Counting Nouns

Structure

The general structure for 个 (gè) and measure words in general is:

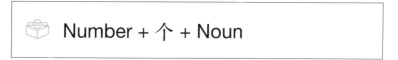

Number + 个 + Noun

Any time you want to state *how many* of a noun in Chinese, you probably need a measure word. First get used to how they are used with 个 (gè).

Examples

* 一 个 人
  yī gè rén
  one person

* 四 个 朋友
  sì gè péngyou
  four friends

* 三 个 苹果手机
  sān gè Píngguǒ shǒujī
  three iPhones

* 五 个 星期
  wǔ gè xīngqī
  five weeks

* 六 个 月
  liù gè yuè
  six months

* 两 个 老婆
  liǎng gè lǎopo
  two wives

* 十 个 男人，七 个 傻，八 个 坏。   *A line from a song*

  Shí gè nánrén, qī gè shǎ, bā gè huài.

  Ten men: seven are fools, and eight are bad.

Omitting the Number

Structure

If the number is one (1), you can omit it and use 个 (gè) by itself. This is similar to "a" or "an" in English, for example in "a person" or "an idiot." (The tone on 个 (gè) is normally somewhat de-emphasized in this usage, but still written as fourth tone. You don't need to stress about it, though.)

Examples

* 他是 个 老外。

  Tā shì gè lǎowài.

  He is a foreigner.

* 我有 个 儿子。

  Wǒ yǒu gè érzi.

  I have a son.

* 她是 个 好老师。

  Tā shì gè hǎo lǎoshī.

  She is a good teacher.

* 你想吃 个 包子吗?

  Nǐ xiǎng chī gè bāozi ma?

  Would you like to eat a stuffed steamed bun?

* 老师，我有 个 问题。

  Lǎoshī, wǒ yǒu gè wèntí.

  Teacher, I have a question.

Similar to

* Age with "sui"
* Measure words for counting

- Measure words in quantity questions
- Measure words with "this" and "that"
- Ordinal numbers with "di"

Other Chinese Grammar Wiki Books

The **Chinese Grammar Wiki** is a free online resource conceived of, designed, and maintained by AllSet Learning. The URL is:

https://resources.allsetlearning.com

Using this resource as a basis, a series of books is being released, based on the complete lists of grammar points by difficulty level:

- Chinese Grammar Wiki BOOK: Elementary
- Chinese Grammar Wiki BOOK: Intermediate (1)
- Chinese Grammar Wiki BOOK: Intermediate (2)
- Chinese Grammar Wiki BOOK: Upper Intermediate (1)
- Chinese Grammar Wiki BOOK: Upper Intermediate (2)

At the same time, shorter, more specialized books (which contain a smaller selection of the above grammar points, organized around a specific theme, with additional explanation where needed) are also being released:

- Chinese Grammar Wiki BOOK: Just the Basics
- Chinese Grammar Wiki BOOK: Mastering *Le*
- Chinese Grammar Wiki BOOK: Comparing
- Chinese Grammar Wiki BOOK: Mastering Complements
- Chinese Grammar Wiki BOOK: Mastering *Shi… De*
- Chinese Grammar Wiki BOOK: Mastering *Ba*
- Chinese Grammar Wiki BOOK: Mastering *Bei*

Look for these books on Amazon.com and the iBooks Store.

Glossary

We strive to avoid unnecessarily technical terms on the Chinese Grammar Wiki, but occasionally it's sort of necessary, and sometimes even useful (yes, really!). So to help you out, we've placed all of the grammatical terms related to Mandarin Chinese in one place. Each term has a page on the wiki with a more complete description, and many pages also have lists of grammar points related to the term.

List of Mandarin Grammar Terms

Action verb — *Also known as:* 动作动词 *(dòngzuò dòngcí) and* 行为动词 *(xíngwéi dòngcí).* Action verbs describe what a subject did, is doing, or will do, physically.

Action-measure complement — *Also known as:* 动量补语 *(dòng-liàng bǔyǔ).* Action-measure complements are words placed after a verb to show the frequency of action.

Adjective — *Also known as:* 形容词 *(xíngróngcí).* Adjectives are the "describing" words of a language. In Chinese, they have some characteristics that they don't have in English.

Adjectival predicate sentence — *Also known as:* 形容词谓语句 *(xíngróngcí wèiyǔ jù) and* 形容词性谓语句 *(xíngróngcí-xìng wèiyǔ jù).* A fancy name for a sentence where the predicate consists of an adjective.

Adverb — *Also known as:* 副词 *(fùcí).* Adverbs are words that modify verbs and adjectives. In Chinese, word order of adverbs is much stricter than in English. Chinese adverbs normally come before the main verb of a sentence, but in some cases come right at the beginning of a sentence.

Adverbial — *Also known as:* 状语 *(zhuàngyǔ).* An adverbial is a sentence element that functions like an adverb, modifying a verb or adjective.

Adverbial phrase — *Also known as:* 副词短语 *(fùcí duǎnyǔ).* An adverbial phrase is a phrase with two or more words that act like an adverb, modifying a verb or adjective.

Affirmative-negative question — *Also known as:* 正反问句 *(zhèng-fǎn wènjù) and alternative questions.* A common way to form questions in Chinese is to first use a verb in the positive, then repeat the same verb in its negative form, similar to how in English we can say, "Do you have money or not?" or "Have you or have you not been to the park?" This sentence pattern feels a lot more natural in Chinese than those admittedly awkward English equivalents, however.

Affix — *Also known as:* 词缀 *(cízhuì).* An affix is a linguistic unit added to the beginning, middle or end of a word to change its meaning (e.g. prefix, infix, suffix).

Aspect — *Also known as:* 动作状态 *(dòngzuò zhuàngtài)* and 语态 *(yǔtài)*. Chinese does not use the concept of formal tenses. Instead, it employs what is called "grammatical aspect." Rather than conjugating its verbs, Chinese uses particles to indicate how a verb works within a particular timeframe, or how the verb relates to the flow of time. The particles most often used to indicate aspect in Chinese are 了 (le), 过 (guo), and 着 (zhe).

Aspectual particle — *Also known as:* 时态助词 *(shítài zhùcí)* and 动态助词 *(dòngtài zhùcí)*. These words are added to verbs to indicate aspect (not the same as tense). The particles most often used to indicate aspect in Chinese are 了 (le), 过 (guo), and 着 (zhe).

Attributive — *Also known as:* 定语 *(dìngyǔ)*. An attributive is the word or phrase that directly precedes the noun it describes. Frequently it is linked to the noun with the structural particle 的 (de).

Auxiliary verb — *Also known as: modal verb,* 助动词 *(zhùdòngcí),* 情态动词 *(qíngtài dòngcí)* and 能愿动词 *(néngyuàn dòngcí)*. Auxiliary verbs are "helping" verbs that come before main verbs and help express a tone or mood. (The word "modal" comes from "mood.") In English, auxiliary verbs include words like "should," "will," and "can," which all change something about the situation and the speaker's attitude. Auxiliary verbs express capability, possibility, necessity, obligation or willingness.

Cardinal number — *Also known as:* 基数词 *(jīshùcí)*. Cardinal numbers are numbers such as 1, 2, or 3 used to indicate quantity. They contrast with ordinal numbers.

Causative verb — *Also known as:* 使令动词 *(shǐlìng dòngcí)* and 使役动词 *(shǐyì dòngcí)*. A causative verb is a kind of verb that is used to indicate that someone or something causes something else to do or be something. In Chinese, 让 (ràng) is a major player in this space.

Complement — *Also known as:* 补语 *(bǔyǔ) and objective complement*. A complement is a word or phrase following a verb (or sometimes an adjective) that provides additional meaning to the verb phrase. Complements are not the same as objects, and can be as short as one character, or practically as long as a sentence. According to A Practical Chinese Grammar for Foreigners, complements "show the duration, quantity, degree, result, direction or possibility of an action; or to illustrate the state, number, degree of a thing." Complements are not a form of flattery (those are compliments); they're much more versatile than that!

Complex sentence — *Also known as:* 复句 *(fùjù)*. A complex sentence is a sentence with one main clause and one or more subordinate clauses.

Conjunction — *Also known as:* 连词 *(liáncí)*. Conjunctions in Chinese do exactly what they do in English: connect things. They help make the transition between ideas smoother and also show the relationships between those ideas.

Content word — *Also known as:* 实词 *(shící).* Content words refer to real objects in the real world, whether solid and palpable, or observable in some other way. These words refer to objects, actions, concepts, and even emotions, which exist in some real way as more than just grammatical tools. Words that serve purely grammatical roles are called function words.

Coverb — *Also known as:* 副动词 *(fùdòngcí)* and 伴动词 *(bàndòngcí).* A coverb is a verb that modifies the main verb of a sentence when used with its own object.

Degree adverb — *Also known as:* 程度副词 *(chéngdù fùcí).* Degree adverbs intensify or in some other way modify the degree of expression of the adjective (or verb).

Degree complement — *Also known as:* 程度补语 *(chéngdù bǔyǔ)* and *complement of degree.* While most complements follow verbs, degree complements very often follow adjectives. They intensify or in some other way modify the degree of expression of the adjective (or verb).

Demonstrative pronoun — *Also known as:* 指示代词 *(zhǐshì dàicí).* A demonstrative pronoun is a pronoun used in the place of a noun and specifies what is being referred to.

Dependent clause — *Also known as:* 从句 *(cóngjù).* A dependent clause is a clause that is dependent on and modifies or supplies with additional information the independent clause. There is a subordinate conjunction at the beginning of dependent clauses causing it to become dependent on independent clauses, even though they have a subject and verb.

Direct object — *Also known as:* 直接宾语 *(zhíjiē bīnyǔ).* A direct object is what is being acted upon, thus receiving the action of a verb. In Chinese grammar, direct objects are often simply referred to as "objects."

Direction complement — *Also known as:* 趋向补语 *(qūxiàng bǔyǔ), directional complement* and *complement of direction.* A *direction complement* is a complement that's to describe the direction of the action of a verb. After the verb which takes the direction complement already has some inherent movement implied, and then adding a direction complement makes clearer where exactly that action is going.

Directional verb — *Also known as:* 趋向动词 *(qūxiàng dòngcí).* Directional verbs can be added to other verbs in a direction complement, illustrating which direction the verb is going.

Directional complement — See **direction complement**

Distinguishing word — *Also known as:* 区别词, *distinguishing words and attributive adjectives.* "Distinguishing words" are rather foreign to the English speaker. On the surface they may seem like regular adjectives, but distinguishing words do not have degree, so they are not modified by adverbs. Unlike normal adjectives, sentences involving distinguishing words use 是 (shì), and usually 的 (de) as well. Common words include the Chinese words for "male," "female," "real," "fake," and colors.

Existential verb — *Also known as:* 存现动词 *(cúnxiàn dòngcí)*. Existential verbs declare the existence or nonexistence of things.

Function word — *Also known as:* 虚词 *(xūcí)*. Function words do not refer to real objects in the real world; rather they serve purely grammatical roles in sentences, drawing relationships and logical connections between the content words in a sentence. Words that refer to real objects in the real world are called content words.

Judgement verb — *Also known as:* 关系动词 *(guānxì dòngcí) and* 判断动词 *(pànduàn dòngcí)*. Judgment verbs are verbs used to express the speaker's judgment. This can be as simple as the verb "to be," but also covers a wide range of other verbs.

Indirect object — *Also known as:* 间接宾语 *(jiànjiē bīnyǔ)*. Indirect objects occur when there are two objects in a sentence. The indirect object is for/to whom/what the action of the verb is done and who/what is receiving the direct object. In Chinese grammar, indirect objects are often referred to as second objects.

Independent clause — *Also known as:* 主句 *(zhǔjù)*. An independent clause is a clause that has a subject and a predicate that modifies the subject, allowing it to stand alone as a sentence.

Independent phrase — *Also known as:* 独立语 *(dúlì yǔ)*. An independent phrase has no subject acting out the verb in the sentence.

Interjection — *Also known as:* 叹词 *(tàncí) and* 感叹词 *(gǎntàncí)*. Express exclamation or various kinds of emotional response.

Interrogative pronoun — See **question word**

Intransitive verb — *Also known as:* 不及物动词 *(bùjíwù dòngcí)*. Intransitive verbs are verbs which take no direct object.

Location word — *Also known as:* 方位名词 *(fāngwèi míngcí)*, 方位词 *(fāng-wèi cí) and noun of locality*. Location nouns are nouns showing direction and location.

Main clause — See **independent clause**

Measure word — *Also known as:* 量词 *(liàngcí) and classifier*. Measure words are used together with numerals to indicate the quantity of a noun, and sometimes even of an action. The general term for "measure word" in linguistics is "classifier," because measure words involve some kind of classification of the noun (or action) being counted.

Mimetic word — See **onomatopoeia**

Modal adverb — *Also known as:* 语气副词 *(yǔqì fùcí) and tone adverb*. Modal adverbs express likelihood with adverbs such as probably, possibly, evidently, certainly, etc.

Modal particle — *Also known as:* 语气助词 *(yǔqì zhùcí),* 语气词 *(yǔqì cí), Sentence-final particle and Sentential particle.* Modal particles are words used at the end of sentences to indicate mood, or attitude. They tend to be neutral tone and hard to translate, but they add a bit of "flavor" to a sentence. See also particles.

Modal verb — See **auxiliary verb**

Negative adverb — *Also known as:* 否定副词 *(fǒudìng fùcí).* Negative adverbs negate verbs and adjectives to make a negative statement. The main ones in Chinese are 不 (bù) and 没 (méi).

Noun — *Also known as:* 名词 *(míngcí).* You may have learned these as "person, place, or thing." Nouns often act as subjects, are modified by adjectives, and can be counted with measure words in Chinese.

Noun measure word — *Also known as:* 名量词 *(míngliàngcí).* As the name suggests, these are measure words that are only used for nouns.

Noun phrase — *Also known as:* 名词短语 *(míngcí duǎnyǔ).* A noun phrase is a phrase with a noun or pronoun as a head word that has any sort of modifier.

Numeral — *Also known as:* 数词 *(shùcí).* A numeral is a symbol that represents a number.

Nominal predicate sentence — *Also known as:* 名词谓语句 *(míngcí wèiyǔjù).* Nominal predicate sentences are sentences with a noun phrase that functions as the main predicate of the sentence.

Object — *Also known as:* 宾语 *(bīnyǔ).* The object is the receiver of the action of the verb.

Onomatopoeia — *Also known as:* 象声词 *(xiàngshēngcí) and* 拟声词 *(nǐshēngcí).* Onomatopoeia are words which represent sounds and noises.

Ordinal number — *Also known as:* 序数词 *(xùshù cí).* Ordinal numbers are numbers used to express rank or sequence. Think "1st," "2nd," etc. Ordinal numbers contrast with cardinal numbers.

Particle — *Also known as:* 助词 *(zhùcí).* Particles are function words that depend on other words or phrases to impart meaning. They're kind of like prepositions, but more abstract. In Chinese, the key ones are aspectual particles (for indicating aspect), structural particles (for indicating relationships between words), and modal particles (for indicating mood). Chinese particles are also special words because they tend to always take the neutral tone.

Passive voice — *Also known as: Passive structure,* 被动结构 *(bèidòng jiégòu),* 被动句式 *(bèidòng jùshì) and* 被动语态 *(bèidòng yǔtài).* "Passive voice" is a grammatical term used to refer to sentences in which the "recipient" of an action (often referred to as the "direct object" or simply "object") becomes the subject of the sentence, and the "doer" of the action is demoted to secondary importance or omitted altogether.

Passive structure — See **passive voice**

Personal pronoun — *Also known as:* 人称代词 *(rénchēng dàicí).* Personal pronouns include 我 (wǒ), 你 (nǐ), 他 (tā), and 她 (tā). To make them plural, all you need to do is add the suffix -们 (-men) to it. Additionally, there is a polite second person form 您 (nín), which cannot normally take the -们 (-men) suffix.

Place noun — *Also known as:* 处所名词 *(chùsuǒ míngcí).* Place nouns are nouns describing the position or place of something.

Place adverb — *Also known as:* 处所副词 *(chùsuǒ fùcí), location adverb, adverb of place and adverb of location.* Place adverbs modify the location of a verbs or adjective.

Placement verb — See **existential verb**

Phrase — *Also known as:* 短语 *(duǎnyǔ) and* 词组 *(cízǔ).* A phrase is a group of words that expresses a concept. It can be focused on fleshing out a particular word, as in a noun phrase or verb phrase. See also clause, which expresses a more complete thought.

Possessive pronoun — *Also known as:* 物主代词 *(wùzhǔ dàicí).* Possessive pronouns take the place of a noun and show ownership.

Potential complement — Verbs can take **potential complements** that indicate whether or not the action is actually possible. They are useful in Chinese to say if an action can take place.

Predicate — *Also known as:* 谓语 *(wèiyǔ).* Predicates are the main verb/verb phrase of a sentence that state something about the subject.

Preposition — *Also known as:* 介词 *(jiècí).* Prepositions are words that indicate location or direction. They are called **pre**positions because they come before the words that they modify.

Prepositional phrase — *Also known as:* 介词短语 *(jiècí duǎnyǔ).* A prepositional phrase is a phrase beginning with a preposition that precedes the word it modifies and clarifies that word's relationship with another word in the sentence.

Pronoun — *Also known as:* 代词 *(dàicí).* Pronouns substitute in for regular nouns and proper nouns to avoid unnecessary repetition of the same words over and over again.

Proper noun — *Also known as:* 专有名词 *(zhuānyǒu míngcí).* A proper noun is specific person, place or thing. Proper nouns are generally capitalized (e.g. John, China, AllSet Learning), both in English and in pinyin.

Psychological verb — *Also known as:* 心理动词 *(xīnlǐ dòngcí) and psych verb.* A psychological verb is a verb that conveys the speaker's mental state or attitude.

Qualitative adjective — *Also known as:* 性质形容词 *(xìngzhì xíngróngcí).* Qualitative adjectives describe the quality or nature of something.

Quantitative phrase — *Also known as:* 数量短语 *(shùliàng duǎnyǔ).* Quantitative phrases express a measurement of amount.

Quantity complement — *Also known as: 数量补语 (shùliàng bǔyǔ), quantitative complement and complement of quantity.* A quantity complement follows a verb and completes the expression of measurement of amount.

Question pronoun — See **question word**

Question word — *Also known as: 疑问代词 (yíwèn dàicí), question pronoun, interrogative pronoun.* A **question word** refers to a special kind of pronoun used to ask questions. These would include 什么 (shénme), 什么时候 (shénme shíhou), 谁 (shéi), 哪儿 (nǎr) / 哪里 (nǎlǐ), 哪个 (nǎge), 为什么 (wèishénme), 怎么 (zěnme). Beginners should pay attention to the placement of question words.

Reduplication — It is one of the great ironies of linguistics that the term for repeating a word is overly repetitive itself. You'd think that the word "duplication" would work just fine, but the linguistic term really is reduplication. In Chinese, verbs and adjectives are often reduplicated.

Relational verb — See **judgement verb**

Result complement — *Also known as: 结果补语 (jiéguǒ bǔyǔ), complement of result, resultative complement and result compound.* Result complements are a kind of verbal complement that appears very frequently in Chinese. Surprisingly enough, they're used to describe the result of a verb.

Scope adverb — *Also known as: 范围副词 (fànwéi fùcí).* Scope adverbs modify and expand a verb or adjective.

Sentence with a nominal predicate — See **nominal predicate sentence**

Sentence with a verbal predicate — *Also known as: 动词谓语句 (dòngcí wèiyǔ jù).* A sentence with a verb as the main element of its predicate is called a sentence with a verbal predicate. This type of sentence is extremely common.

Sentence with an adjectival predicate — See **adjectival predicate sentence**

Sentence with a subject-predicate structure as predicate — *Also known as: 主谓谓语句 (zhǔ-wèi wèiyǔ jù).*

Sentence-final particle — See **modal particle**

Sentential particle — See **modal particle**

Separable verb — *Also known as: 离合词 (líhécí) and verb-object phrase.* "Separable verbs" get their name from their ability to "separate" into two parts (a verb part and an object part), with other words in between. In fact, you could also simply call separable verbs "verb-object phrases."

Subject — *Also known as: 主语 (zhǔyǔ).* A subject is a noun or pronoun that the sentence centers around. It is the actor of the verb and is what something is said about.

Subject-predicate construction — *Also known as: 主谓结构 (zhǔ-wèi jiégòu).* The subject-predicate construction consists of a subject and a predicate, and may be part of a larger sentence, or may serve as a sentence on its own.

Subject-predicate sentence — *Also known as:* 主谓句 *(zhǔ-wèi jù).* A sentence composed of a subject and a predicate. The vast majority of sentences fit this description.

Subordinate clause — See **dependent clause**

State complement — *Also known as:* 状态补语 *(zhuàngtài bǔyǔ),* 情态补语 *(qíngtài bǔyǔ) and complement of state.* State complements describe an achieved state of an action. State complements are usually adjective phrases (adverb + adjective) but can take the form of verbal phrases, subject-predicate phrase or other complements. State complements that are adjective phrases often look the same as degree complements and thus often lumped together with degree complements in textbooks.

Stative adjective — *Also known as:* 状态形容词 *(zhuàngtài xíngróngcí).* A stative adjective is an adjective describing a relatively unchanging or permanent condition/state.

Stative verb — *Also known as:* 状态动词 *(zhuàngtài dòngcí),* 静态动词 *(jìngtài dòngcí), state verb and static verb.* A stative verb is a verb describing a relatively unchanging or permanent condition/state. Stative verbs in Mandarin are usually translated as adjectives in English.

Structural particle — *Also known as:* 结构助词 *(jiégòu zhùcí).* A structural particle is a function word that denotes the structural/grammatical relationship between elements of a sentence.

Time adverb — *Also known as:* 时间副词 *(shíjiān fùcí).* Adverbs of time express the when, how long, or how often of a verb.

Time phrase — *Also known as:* 时间短语 *(shíjiān duǎnyǔ).* A time phrase occurs before the verb phrase and indicates the when, how long, or how often of a situation.

Time noun — *Also known as:* 时间名词 *(shíjiān míngcí),* 时间词 *(shíjiāncí), time nominal and temporal noun.* Time nouns are nouns that indicate a point in time.

Time-measure complement — *Also known as:* 时量补语 *(shí-liàng bǔyǔ).* Time-measure complements show the state or duration of an action.

Tone adverb — See **modal adverb**

Topic-comment structure — *Also known as:* 主题句 *(zhǔtí-jù),* 主题结构 *(zhǔtí jiégòu),* 主题评论结构 *(zhǔtí-pínglùn jiégòu),* 主题述题结构 *(zhǔtí-shùtí jiégòu) and* 主题评述结构 *(zhǔtí-píngshù jiégòu).* A topic-comment structure is an alternative to the typical subject-predicate sentence structure, whereby a topic (or theme) is followed by the speaker's comment on that topic. The topic is not the "doer" (subject) of the sentence, but rather sets the scope of the comments (some thoughts related to the topic).

Transitive verb — *Also known as:* 及物动词 *(jíwù dòngcí).* A transitive verb is an verb which takes a direct object.

Verb — *Also known as: 动词 (dòngcí).* Verbs are the "action" words which make up the predicates of most sentences, but may also simply indicate relationships, changes, or mental activity rather than physical actions. Verbs may take objects, and can also be reduplicated in Chinese. They can be negated, as well as modified by particles.

Verb measure word — *Also known as: 动量词 (dòng liàngcí), verbal measure word and verbal classifier.* A verb measure word accompanies the number of times a verb occurred to count the frequency or re-occurrence of an action.

Verb phrase — *Also known as: 动词短语 (dòngcí duǎnyǔ).* A verb phrase is a phrase with a verb as a head word that has any sort of modifier. It commonly includes modal verbs before it and objects after it.

Verbal predicate sentence — See **sentence with a verbal predicate**

Acknowledgments

The Chinese Grammar Wiki may have been pioneered by AllSet Learning, but it would not be possible without the hard work of many selfless individuals, including AllSet Learning interns, students, teachers, and regular users. Thank you!

AllSet Interns

· Donna Yee · Lucas Simons · Hugh Grigg · Greg McAndrews · Jonathan Pope · Pavel Dvorak · Parry Cadwallader · Jack Overstreet · Dan Emery · Erick Garcia · Mei Tong · Ben Slye · Brandon Sanchez · Logan Pauley · Ashlyn Weber · Michelle Birkenfeldt · Zach Herzog · Jazlyn Akaka · Salomé Vergne · Natalie Kuan · Jack Du · Erick Garcia · Cai Qingyang · Michael Moore · Liza Fowler · Mike Blood · Jacob Rodgers · Dominic Pote · Amani Core · Michelle Guerra · Amanda Gilbride · Callan Mossman · Jenna Salisbury ·

Special thanks to interns Michelle Guerra, Amanda Gilbride, and Callan Mossman for all the excruciating pinyin and typo checking they did.

Volunteer Editors

Some of these editors did tons of work on their own, while others emailed in issues they found. We thank them all for the hard work and valuable contributions!

· Nicholas Fiorentini · Noémi Németh · Betsy · HuaWei · Kryby · Jay · Luolimao · Trackpick · Morris · Philip Harding · Gintaras Valentukonis ·

AllSet Teachers and Staff

· 陈世霜 (Chén Shìshuāng) · 刘倖倖 (Liú Xìngxìng) · 赵以华 (Zhào Yǐhuá) · 于翠 (Yú Cuì) · 杨仁君 (Yáng Rénjùn) · 毛思平 (Máo Sīpíng) · 吴蒙蒙 (Wú Méngméng) · 贾贝茜 (Jiǎ Bèixī) · Parry Cadwallader · Michael Moore · John Pasden ·

Although many AllSet Learning employees have worked on the wiki over the years, both part-time and full-time staff, a special shout-out goes to 陈世霜 (Chén Shìshuāng), who has toiled tirelessly on the wiki behind the scenes for years without complaining. This print book is your victory as well!

Sincere thanks to Parry Cadwallader for making both the original wiki itself as well as the ebook version of the Chinese Grammar Wiki possible technically, with very little extra production work needed from the academic team. A big thank you also to Adam Zydney for all the layout work that went into creating the print version.

Other Credits

The Chinese Grammar Wiki website and ebook both make use of the **Silk** icon set **FamFamFam.com**. The Chinese Grammar Wiki BOOK (print edition) uses a "structure" icon from **Pixeden.com**, as well as several icons from **Icomoon.io**.

References

This page is a bibliography for the Chinese Grammar Wiki. It lists all sources referenced extensively when researching the content of the Chinese Grammar Wiki grammar points.

- Chen, Ru 陈如, and Xiaoya Zhu 朱晓亚. *Hanyu Changyong Geshi 330 Li* 汉语常用格式 330 例 *[Common Chinese Patterns 330]*. Beijing: Beijing Foreign Languages Printing House, 2010. Print.

- Fang, Yuqing 房玉清. *Shiyong Hanyu Yufa* 实用汉语语法 *[A Practical Chinese Grammar]*. Beijing: Beijing Yuyan Daxue Chubanshe, 2008. Print.

- Herzberg, Qin Xue, and Larry Herzberg. *Basic Patterns of Chinese Grammar: A Student's Guide to Correct Structures and Common Errors*. Berkeley, CA: Stone Bridge, 2011. Print.

- Ho, Yong. *Intermediate Chinese*. New York: Hippocrene, 2004. Print.

- Li, Charles N., and Sandra A. Thompson. *Mandarin Chinese: A Functional Reference Grammar*. Berkeley: U of California, 1981. Print.

- Li, Dejin 李德津, and Meizhen Cheng 程美珍, eds. *Waiguoren Shiyong Hanyu Yufa* 外国人实用汉语语法 *[A Practical Chinese Grammar for Foreigners]*. Beijing: Beijing Yuyan Daxue Chubanshe, 1998. Print.

- Li, Luxing 李禄兴, Ling Zhang 张玲, and Juan Zhang 张娟. *Hanyu Yufa Baixiang Jianglian: Chuzhongji* 汉语语法百项讲练：初中级 *[Chinese Grammar–Broken Down Into 100 Items]*. Beijing: Beijing Language and Culture UP, 2011. Print.

- Li, Xiaoqi 李晓琪, ed. *Xiandai Hanyu Xuci Shouce* 现代汉语虚词手册 *[Modern Chinese Function Words Handbook]: A Guide to Function Words in Modern Chinese*. Beijing: Beijing Daxue Chubanshe, 2003. Print.

- Liu, Delian 刘德联, and Xiaoyu Liu 刘晓雨. *Hanyu Kouyu Changyong Jushi Lijie* 汉语口语常用句式例解 *[Exemplification of Common Sentence Patterns in Spoken Chinese]*. Ed. Liwen Song 宋立文. Beijing: Beijing Daxue Chubanshe, 2005. Print.

- Liu, Xun 刘珣, ed. *Xin Shiyong Hanyu Keben* 新实用汉语课本 *[New Practical Chinese Reader Textbook 1]*. Beijing: Beijing Language and Culture UP, 2002. Print.

- Liu, Xun 刘珣. *Xin Shiyong Hanyu Keben* 新实用汉语课本 *[New Practical Chinese Reader Textbook 2]*. Beijing: Beijing Language and Culture UP, 2002. Print.

- Liu, Xun 刘珣. *Xin Shiyong Hanyu Keben* 新实用汉语课本 *[New Practical Chinese Reader Textbook 3]*. Beijing: Beijing Language and Culture UP, 2003. Print.

- Liu, Yuehua 刘月华, Wenyu Pan 潘文娱, and Wei Gu 故桦. *Shiyong Xiandai Hanyu Yufa* 实用现代汉语语法 *[Practical Modern Chinese Grammar]*. Beijing: Shangwu Yinshuguan Chuban, 2001. Print.

- Liu, Yuehua, and Tao-chung Yao. *Zhongwen Tingshuo Duxie* 中文听说读写 *[Integrated Chinese Textbook Simplified Characters Level 1 Part 2]*. 3rd ed. Boston: Cheng & Tsui, 2009. Print.

- Liu, Yuehua, and Tao-chung Yao. *Zhongwen Tingshuo Duxie* 中文听说读写 *[Integrated Chinese Textbook Simplified Characters Level 2 Part 2]*. 3rd ed. Boston: Cheng & Tsui, 2009. Print.

- Liu, Yuehua, and Tao-chung Yao. *Zhongwen Tingshuo Duxie* 中文听说读写 *[Integrated Chinese Textbook Simplified Characters Level 1 Part 1]*. 3rd ed. Boston: Cheng & Tsui, 2009. Print.

- Liu, Yuehua, and Tao-chung Yao. *Zhongwen Tingshuo Duxie* 中文听说读写 *[Integrated Chinese Textbook Simplified Characters Level 2 Part 1]*. 3rd ed. Boston: Cheng & Tsui, 2009. Print.

- Lü, Shuxiang 吕叔湘, comp. *Xiandai Hanyu Babai Ci* 现代汉语八百词 *[800 Modern Chinese Words]*. Beijing: Shangwu Yinshuguan, 1980. Print.

- Ma, Jing-heng Sheng, and Claudia Ross. *Modern Mandarin Chinese Grammar: A Practical Guide*. London: Routledge, 2006. Print.

- Mu, Ling, Rongzhen Li, and Peisong Xu. *Chinese Usage Dictionary*. Center for Language Study, Yale University, 2004. Web.

- "Qingwen." Podcast audio content. *ChinesePod*. Web.

- Ross, Claudia. *Schaum's Outline of Chinese Grammar*. New York: McGraw-Hill, 2004. Print.

- Teng, Wen-Hua. *Yufa!: A Practical Guide to Mandarin Chinese Grammar*. London: Hodder Education, 2011. Print.

- *Xiandai Hanyu Xuci Lishi* 现代汉语虚词例释 *[Modern Chinese Function Words Examples and Explanations]*. Beijing: Shangwu Yinshuguan, 1957. Print.

- Yip, Po-ching, and Don Rimmington. *Chinese: An Essential Grammar*. London: Routledge, 1997. Print.

- Yip, Po-ching, Don Rimmington, Xiaoming Zhang, and Rachel Henson. *Basic Chinese: A Grammar and Workbook*. London: Routledge, 1998. Print.

- Zhang, Jing 张婧, ed. *Yufa Jingjiang Jinglian* 语法精讲精练 *[Practicing HSK Grammar]*. 1st ed. Beijing: Sinolingua, 2008. Print.

- Zhu, Xiaoxing 朱晓星, ed. *Jianming Hanyu Yufa Xuexi Shouce* 简明汉语语法学习手册 *[Simple Chinese Grammar Study Handbook]: Chinese Grammar without Tears*. Beijing: Beijing Daxue Chubanshe, 2002. Print.

Made in the USA
Lexington, KY
29 April 2019